Memories of North and West Sutherland

compiled by

Christopher J. Uncles

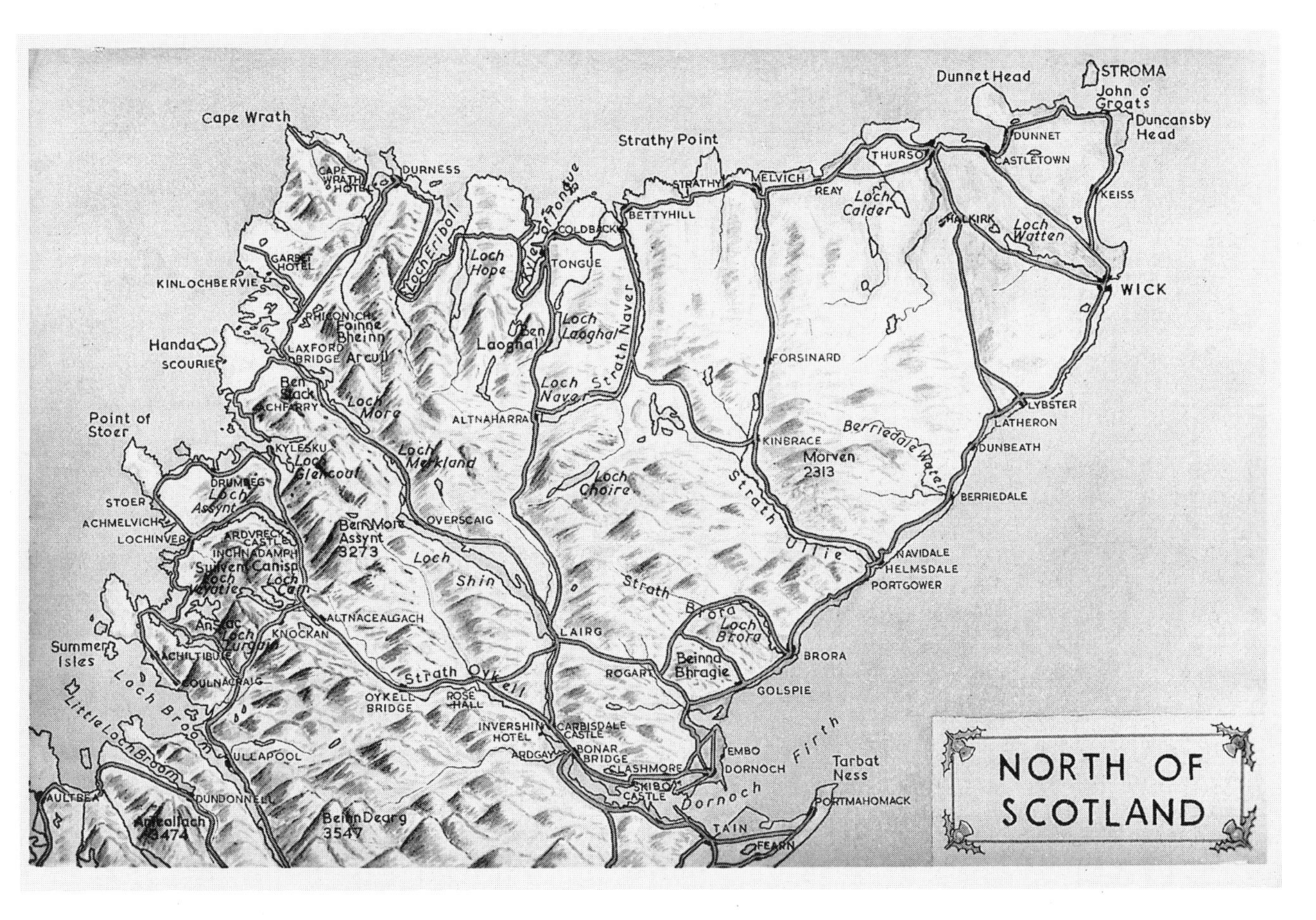

North by North-West. Dr (later Sir) Frank Fraser Darling's description of the Highland landscape as a 'man-made desert' is as apt today as it was when he penned these words in 1947. Bounded by Melvich, Kinbrace, Lairg, Altnacealgach and Lochinver, this book provides a portrait of these 'empty lands' of Sutherland.

Stenlake Publishing
2003

FOREWORD

The date of 6 June 1966 is indelibly printed on my memory. On that morning 37 years ago my wife and I left the Royal Hotel at Cromarty, motored around the Firth (no causeway in those days), and eventually crossed the Kyle of Sutherland at Bonar Bridge. Lairg lay before us, but our ultimate destination was Kinlochbervie in the far north-west. The Garbet Hotel, where we had arranged to stay for the week, had been totally destroyed by fire the previous August, but just ten months later a new building had risen from the ashes. We were among the very first guests to be received at the rebuilt hotel. North of the Kylesku ferry the roads, sometimes bordered with the brilliant yellow gorse of early summer, were single-track and tortuous, and often poorly served with passing places. Frequently the strip of grass which grew down the centre of the track dividing two narrow widths of tarmac dusted the oil sump – and these were the main 'A' classification roads. Modern, wider roads have now replaced the ones over which we then travelled, but everywhere traces of decaying tarmac are still plainly visible in the encroaching moorland.

For its size Great Britain has long been recognised as possessing a greater variety of classically distinctive land types than anywhere else in the world, and Sutherland is a land like no other. A number of differing influences, both natural and man-made, have shaped not only features of the landscape, but also all aspects of commercial and economic development in this north-western corner of mainland Britain, which is rich in history and yet largely bereft of people today.

Divided into three sections (the first of which includes a short introduction), *Memories of North and West Sutherland* is a portrayal in old photographs and postcards of a unique landscape from late Victorian times until the Second World War.

Christopher J. Uncles

ACKNOWLEDGEMENTS

All the photographs used in this book have been selected from my own collection, unless otherwise attributed. For additional photographs, for responses to often obscure queries and for help willingly given, my grateful thanks are due especially to: Gilbert B. Archer (Chairman, Tods of Orkney Ltd.); Graham and Elizabeth Best of Elizabeth's Cafe (Clachan); Peter Burr of Tongue; Alastair Cormack of Kirkwall; Mike and Kai Geldard (The Crask Inn); Nicholas Gorton (Inver Lodge Hotel, Lochinver); Robert Grieves of Paisley; Michael Keitch (Strathtongue Old Manse); Norman A. Macaskill OBE of Lochinver; Neil Mackay of Kirtomy; Willie Morrison of Dingwall; Bruce Sandison and the Skerray Historical Association; The Grosvenor Estate; and The Wick Society.

As before, the all-important technical and production aspects were handled by my wife Angela and Oliver van Helden of Stenlake Publishing.

First published in the United Kingdom, 2003,
by Stenlake Publishing
Telephone / Fax: 01290 551122

ISBN 1 84033 233 6

ROADS BEYOND LAIRG

Sutherland, one of the two most northerly mainland counties, spans the breadth of Scotland, her western shores washed by the Atlantic Ocean, and those to the north and east by the Pentland Firth and the North Sea respectively. Much of the hinterland consists of rugged mountains, immense tracts of bare moorland, blanket bog and lochans – a huge area where sporting lodges, and the deer upon which they depend, are more likely to be encountered than human beings. The fjord-like western seaboard is deeply indented by numerous lochs or arms of the sea, producing stunning glimpses of savage beauty at every turn. Where sparkling rivers run to the sea there are rocky, island-studded bays, cliffs and isolated sea stacks and sandy beaches (often totally deserted) upon which even so much as a footprint might appear as a gross intrusion. Viewed from differing vantage points, groups of mysterious, weirdly-shaped mountains peer above the skyline presenting a panorama of ever-changing shapes which may confuse the traveller on the move. Always vast, this landscape can in turn seem intimidating, or by a weather change, assume a mantle of breathtaking beauty. Such features are the embodiment of 'life at the edge' in the magical west.

The great cliffs of Clò Mòr stand over 900 feet high (the loftiest in mainland Britain), and together with exquisite sandy beaches, rocky bays and headlands look north to the far-distant Faroe Islands. Orkney and Shetland lie to the east across the Pentland Firth from neighbouring Caithness. Along this rugged and spectacular coastline, small and scattered communities huddle together as if for protection against the encircling and often tempestuous seas; the reason for their very existence here will become apparent.

The total land mass of the whole county amounts to nearly 1.3 million acres, an area which in 1901 supported a population of only 21,550. At the census 60 years later, a reduced figure of 13,442 confirmed a continuing trend of decline and gave a ratio of over 96 acres per head of population.

Sutherland has no large towns; indeed North and West Sutherland have nothing which could be even remotely described as a town of any description. Nevertheless Lairg parish – with a population of 1,000 or so inhabitants in 1900 – became a place of supreme economic importance to the whole county because roads, which converged from all points of the compass around the south-eastern end of Loch Shin, facilitated the movement of travellers, goods and produce, and Her Majesty's Royal Mail over a wide area. This picture of *c.*1906 shows the nucleus of the village (which then had a history of less than 100 years), with Lairg Lodge situated on rising ground above Loch Shin.

The 3rd Duke of Sutherland (1828–1892) kept abreast with the ideas and technology of his times; he both developed and improved his huge Sutherland estate by reclaiming land, building shooting lodges and by taking more than a passing interest in the fledgling railway companies which were pushing their lines north from Inverness. Seeing an opportunity to open up the interior and bring prosperity to an area lacking facilities, he was instrumental in influencing the course of the iron road to Caithness on an inland detour through Lairg and Strath Fleet when the favoured option was the easier, less expensive and more direct east coast route. Lairg Station (seen here prior to 1914 and located nearly two miles from the village), opened in 1868 and emphasised the importance of Lairg as the distributive centre for the whole of Sutherland.

Lairg lamb sales, 1939. Commencing in 1894 from modest beginnings when Perth auctioneers conducted the first sale on the hotel farm, the August sale of sheep and lambs on the hill adjoining the station is now claimed as the largest one-day event of its kind in Europe, with up to 40,000 animals changing hands. Hardly surprising, perhaps, as vast areas round and about were cleared of people so that Cheviot sheep could thrive – and they have!

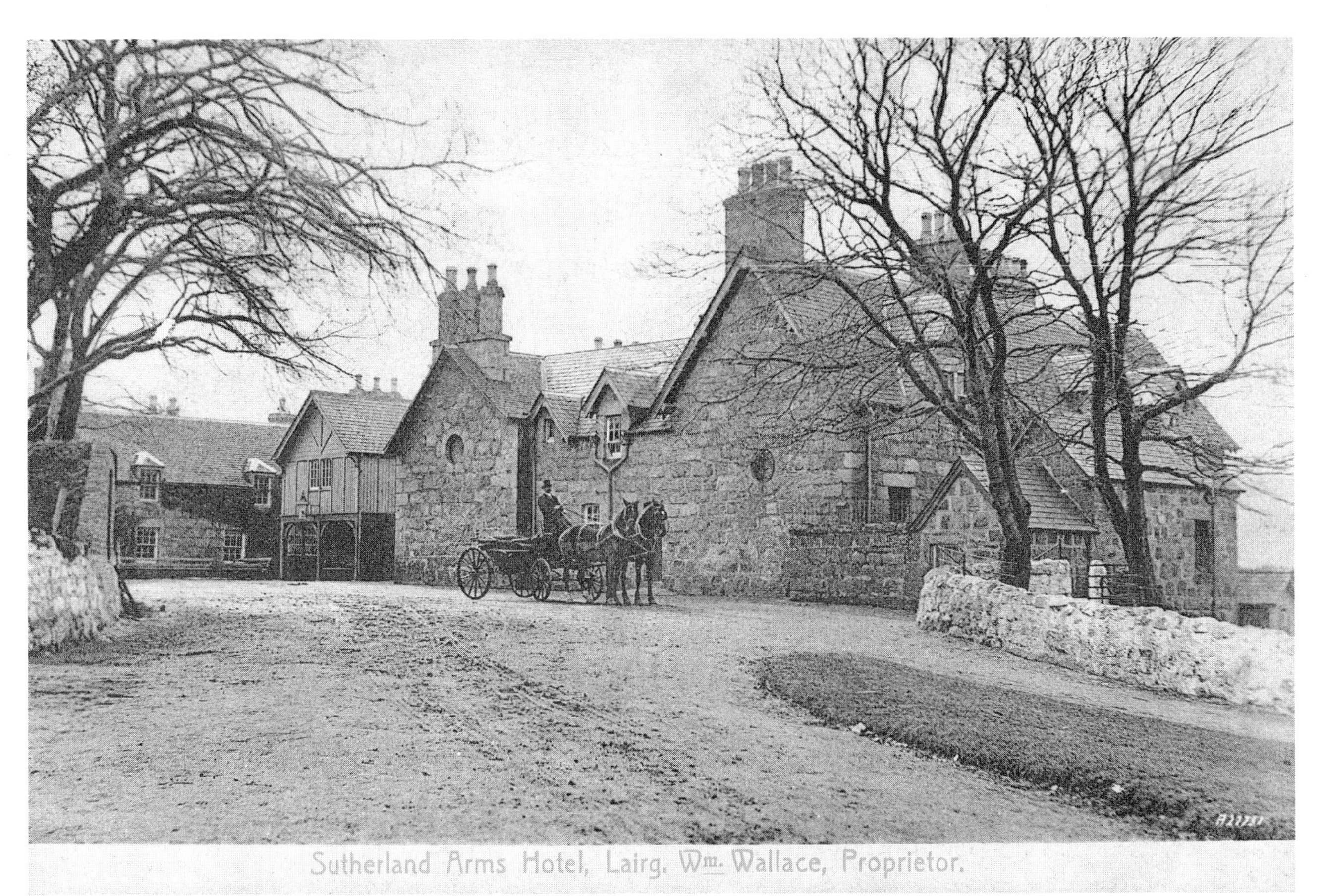

Dating largely from 1864, the somewhat rambling Sutherland Arms Hotel incorporates the site of a modest inn which stood here some 50 years earlier. Sutherland is a county where fishing is taken *most* seriously, and the hotel by Loch Shin soon became a well-known venue for the sporting gentry – although at the time of writing it presents a sad appearance being closed and boarded-up. This postcard (*c*.1906) dates from the proprietorship of William Wallace of Oban; more will be said shortly concerning his associated transport and mail activities, which over time eventually grew to become the Sutherland Transport & Trading Co. Ltd. This is an appropriate point to look in more detail at three routes beyond Lairg over which passengers, goods and the mail were conveyed to the farthest points of North and West Sutherland during the closing years of Queen Victoria's reign. A travel guide of 1884 sheds some interesting insights on not only how people travelled in those days, but also the distances commonly covered on foot. The three routes briefly described below were all former 'green roads' over which the old-time drovers moved their cattle and sheep to the trysts further south.

Lairg–Altnaharra–Tongue: 'Mail-carts depart Tu. Th. Sat. about 6.30 a.m. Fare 7/6d.' About 1819, the famous engineer Thomas Telford was charged with the responsibility of upgrading this route by constructing the many single-span bridges required, although I doubt whether he considered 'The Crask' to be one of his most challenging assignments. Initially running alongside Loch Shin, the course of the road branches up Strath Tirry through open country and makes a gradual climb past the isolated Crask Inn to The Crask (869 feet) before making an equally gradual descent through Strath Vagastie to the Altnaharra Inn, twenty miles from Lairg. The change-house there ensured refreshment for travellers, and a rest or change of team for the toiling horses. The Tongue Hotel lay seventeen miles further to the north, and the journey to the coast was completed only after skirting the full length of Loch Loyal.

However, those on foot making for Durness in the far north-west faced a very different experience. They could leave the coach at Altnaharra and trudge the seventeen miles through lonely Strathmore to the head of Loch Hope, where at Cashel Dhu light refreshment was obtainable at a shepherd's house and the Strathmore River could be crossed by a small ferry. Once across, the track began a sharp four mile ascent to a height of 716 feet above sea level (where the whole expanse of Loch Eriboll could be seen) before descending by a zigzag path towards the small kirk by the roadside. Here, the travel guide asserts 'carriages continue along the road, and proceed all the way round the head of the loch'.

A small sailing-boat ferry also crossed Loch Eriboll, but by road Durness still lay fifteen miles distant, and those using this particular route from Lairg must have felt they had travelled to the end of the earth to reach their destination, perhaps with good reason! But there was an easier, alternative route for those with 15/- to spare.

Lairg–Scourie and Durness: 'Mail-cart to Scourie and Durness daily, about 6.30 a.m. Fare to Scourie 12/-; Durness about 15/-.' This road to the north-west accompanies Loch Shin throughout its length and winds around a series of lochs in the Reay Forest before reaching Laxford Bridge (37 miles). At that point Scourie lies seven miles to the south and Durness nineteen miles to the north. The section from Lairg to Laxford Bridge was a 'destitution road' built in 1850/1 to provide local employment after the disastrous years of the potato famine: coaching stables for the change of horses were located at Overscaig and Achfary. This route had also been an historic drove-road, the cattle being brought together on the gathering grounds around Laxford Bridge before being driven this way via Lairg to Bonar Bridge and the south.

Lairg–Lochinver: 'Mail-cart daily from Lairg village about 6 a.m., reaching Lochinver between 2 p.m. and 3 p.m.; Fare 12/-'. Completed in the 1820s, this road developed from another drovers' track, this time from Assynt through Ledmore and Strath Oykel to Bonar Bridge. The strath is a vast, broad valley, approached from Lairg in a south-westerly direction. Important inns were, and still are, at Oykel Bridge and Altnacealgach on this 49 mile journey to Lochinver.

The Sutherland Transport & Trading Co. Ltd.: By the last two decades of the nineteenth century, improvements to the transport infrastructure were proving immensely beneficial in sustaining and enhancing the quality of life throughout Sutherland, especially in certain remote coastal communities whose previous dependence on supplies delivered by sea had been almost total. Lairg now became the natural focus for trade and services – and a conduit for news – for the whole county. Through the busy railhead livestock were despatched south, while flowing in the opposite direction came goods of all description and, increasingly, curious tourists for whom a little-known corner of Britain was now accessible. Some came to walk and climb the hills, others to stalk deer, while yet more arrived to fish the waters of sea, river and loch. The money spent at hotels (and, more often at modest inns) for accommodation, and the fees paid to hire the services of ghillies and stalkers sustained employment, and became mainstays of the local economy.

Against such a background a small transport company was established in Lairg, and from humble beginnings the business eventually grew to become the Sutherland Transport & Trading Co. Ltd., a company which cast its net of trading activities both within and far beyond the borders of Sutherland. The affectionately-known ST&T was destined to become a household name, and would claim a special place in the hearts of those, especially in far-off places, who eagerly awaited the arrival of the company's vehicles bringing tourists, goods and services and news from afar.

The origins of these developments go back to *c.*1878 when Messrs Gray and Murray (of Colaboll and Achinduich respectively) formed a partnership in that name for conveying passengers and mail by horse and coach to Lochinver, Scourie and Tongue. The dawn of the twentieth century saw the trading name change to 'Coaching Company', and shortly thereafter to 'Sutherland Motor Traffic Co. Ltd.'. During 1905 William Wallace of Oban introduced the first motor vehicle on the mail routes, and the registration of a Daimler wagonette in his name on 24 October that year is possibly the earliest reference to his activities in Lairg. He motorised the mail business completely, and introduced a fleet of private hire cars which, complete with driver, could be rented to landowners for the use of well-to-do guests staying at their sporting lodges.

By 1910 the commercial fleet consisted of about a dozen open wagonettes which each carried five passengers (who were totally exposed to the elements) and incorporated a rear platform suitable for the conveyance of such diverse items as calves, lobsters and mail. Two classes of tickets were issued, and second class fares were obliged to push on the braes if required. In 1920 the company's name changed to the Sutherland Transport & Trading Co. Ltd., and an institution was born.

There is much more that could be said about the company, but space does not permit. Solid expansion followed the acquisition of the ST&T by the Duke of Westminster's Estates in 1951 when the range of activities increased, and with over 100 people directly employed the company was for many years the largest employer in Sutherland. Sadly, unfavourable legislation and changing times resulted in the dissolution of the company (which had been ailing for some years) in 1994. The essential core business of carrying passengers and mails established back in 1878 still continues to this day, but by means of that modern lifeline to distant communities, the postbus.

Motoring under difficulties near Lairg.

Motoring under difficulties near Lairg

In the relatively gentle hills around Lairg a blizzard can result in deep drifts, quickly putting the landscape under a blanket of snow, blotting out landmarks and transforming the scene into a winter wonderland. While today one might reasonably expect Highland Regional Council to be out and about with their gritting vehicles and de-icing equipment, a century ago the responsibility for keeping the roads open rested on men wielding shovels. These postcards show NS 61, a 16 h.p. Albion wagonette, in thick snow on different occasions. *Left:* The severity of the problem can be judged by the extent of the snow-cutting which was recorded as being 'one mile and two furlongs in length'. Hard work for the shovellers! *Right:* This same vehicle (newly registered to William Wallace of the Sutherland Arms Hotel in August 1906 and held by him until November 1910) could be fitted temporarily with a cover in order to provide protection from the elements, if required. One suspects that such conditions were all in a day's work for Wallace, who had revolutionised the mail-carrying enterprise. In November 1907 *Motor World* observed that 'his keen business methods and untiring energy should ensure the success of this venture'.

Busy scenes at Lairg Post Office in the early 1960s as ST&T buses load before driving off to destinations which included Tongue, Bettyhill, Kinlochbervie and Lochinver. On this occasion the Albion (top) was bound for Scourie while the Bedford was being made ready for Durness. Passengers were carried in the forward section, while mail and goods occupied the remainder. Typical loads might include milk and eggs, general supplies, requisites from the chemist, laundry, and newspapers and parcels which had arrived by rail at Lairg Station for onward delivery. (Photographs taken by Robert Grieves and reproduced here with his kind permission.)

A backward glance. This is the receding view of Lairg those bound for Tongue or Laxford Bridge would have seen *c*.1905; needless to say the intervening years have seen much change and development. The road to these destinations divides at Colaboll, but initially shares a common course by Loch Shin, passing close to Lairg Lodge.

Lairg Lodge, *c*.1900. Built by the 3rd Duke of Sutherland in the 1870s and prominently overlooking the village and Loch Shin, the building exemplifies and incorporates all the features so typical of grandiose Victorian sporting lodge architecture. A Mecca for shooting (deer, grouse, partridge and snipe) and fishing (salmon and brown trout), where the every need of guests would be attended to by a large staff. Sir William Edgar Horne, a financier, purchased the Lairg Estate from the Duke in 1919 and proved an enlightened laird, installing electricity both for the lodge and the village, as well as making a number of progressive agricultural and industrial improvements which, during his stewardship, ensured full employment and continuing prosperity for the district.

The all-important motor house, built by the Duke of Sutherland, once stood below the lodge. Motors, no less than guests, required proper accommodation, care and attention – and, in the early days, their own staff.

Windswept bent protrudes through the frozen ground; a vehicle with snow-clogged wheels; men, some with shovels, others with sacks. Every picture tells a story, but plainly the post for Tongue looks to be subject to delay on this occasion, and one can only speculate that the mailbags are, perhaps, being transferred to another (open) vehicle. Hardly surprising that in winter many drivers charged with the responsibility of carrying the mail refused to leave Lairg without a full hip-flask, or that after a particularly fraught journey they frequently failed to appear on time!

The Crask Inn on the Altnaharra road described on page five may even predate the Telford era. Built originally to provide shelter for those on foot, many must have been thankful to have found protection here, especially in winter. *Above:* A motorist staying the night in July 1934 noted on the reverse of this photograph disappointment that Ben Klibreck (3,154 feet) was obscured by cloud. *Below:* Winter snow at Crask – a more recent photograph of the inn where Mike and Kai Geldard welcome travellers today. I will say more subsequently about Altnaharra, but meanwhile return to Loch Shin and the road to Laxford Bridge. (Photograph taken by Mike Geldard and reproduced here with his kind permission.)

This motorist seen by the northern shore of Loch Shin in the 1930s may not have been aware that he was near the scene of a brave experiment in land reclamation which took place between 1873 and 1877 at the foot of Strath Tirry between Colaboll and Shinness. Using hundreds of men and a startlingly-shaped new plough (known as 'the Duke's Toothpick') to clear boulders and roots, Kenneth Murray of Geanies, acting on behalf of the Duke of Sutherland, drained and fenced nearly 2,000 acres in order to grow crops of barley, oats and turnips. Sadly, these efforts ultimately proved uneconomic. An obelisk commemorating 'the Great Plough' and Kenneth Murray stands on the hillside above the Shinness loop road. Our motorist may also have seen a small, corrugated structure known locally as 'the Duke's tea hut', where the Duke could observe progress while taking refreshment.

Situated some sixteen miles from Lairg, the Overscaig Hotel looks out across Loch Shin and stands on the historic droving route from Laxford Bridge over which sheep and cattle were driven to markets at Ardgay and Dingwall. In late Victorian times the inn maintained coaching stables where teams of horses could be refreshed and changed. This photograph well illustrates the structural additions made over the years; even so the present building quite possibly stands on the site of a much earlier hostelry.

Seen here *c.*1909, Loch Merkland Lodge lies beside a river and loch of the same name two and a half miles beyond Loch Shin. Estate-related activities benefit the local economy greatly by providing employment, thereby helping to sustain small communities. Some explanation of this work may be enlightening.

The word 'mountain' is seldom used by indigenous Scots, and throughout the length of the land from the Cheviots to Cranstackie, locals tend to refer to almost any tract of treeless, barren terrain (regardless of height and whether snow-topped or otherwise) as simply 'the hill'. 'It's a fine day for the hill' is commonly heard on a day of good visibility. These hills, particularly the upland areas of the Highlands, are both a fragile environment and home to large numbers of red deer. Between 1972 and 1992 numbers rose from an estimated 185,000 animals to over 300,000, largely concentrated on open hillsides – a number considered quite unsustainable. Deer are capable of causing severe damage to grass and heather, farming and forestry, so overall numbers need to be kept in check, and the weaker, poorer specimens culled for the health of the general herd. Shooting lodges are widely distributed throughout the Highlands, and the accommodation provided ranges from the sumptuous to the purely functional, while others possess the creature comforts more often associated with a Victorian orphanage. Among the varied outbuildings might be one or more deer or game larders, and stabling for the ponies. Well-managed estates can charge substantial sums of money to those who come north for the stalking, although few estates admit to breaking-even financially.

A typical day at a lodge during the season will commence with a hearty breakfast, for the next meal will be twelve hours away. In the intervening time, the prospect of a twenty mile hike over rough terrain in less than ideal weather conditions is a distinct possibility. The head stalker whom you will accompany will be an experienced man who will take control of every aspect of the day's activities. He knows the lie of the land like the back of his hand, he will decide the route to be taken, when to walk or crawl on all fours, and where you stop for your lunchtime 'piece'. He knows, too, the likely places where deer gather, will spy out the landscape, choose the animal to be despatched, and bring hunter and hunted closely and silently together for, hopefully, one decisive shot. A 'kill' will be brought off the hill by pony or, more often today, by a cross-country vehicle.

At the day's end back at the lodge, a couple of drams and a long hot bath beckon – and a chance to catch up with the experiences of others over dinner. Should the stalk have been unsuccessful, there is always the opportunity for another attempt amid the high hills tomorrow.

LOCH MORE LODGE, shewing LOCH MORE. LOCH STACK & BEN ARKLE.

At the far end of Loch More are Lochmore Lodge and Achfary, which form the centre of the 95,000 acre Reay Forest Estate, owned by the Grosvenor Trusts. As long ago as 1847 Earl Grosvenor (who succeeded his father in 1869 and was created 1st Duke of Westminster five years later) had taken a liking to this area following a visit to the remote and recently built Gobernuisgach Lodge, when, in the company of the Duke of Sutherland's son and a Mr Ellis, he made an excursion here from Dunrobin. Three years later he built Lochstack Lodge and was the first to pass along the Lairg to Laxford 'destitution road' when completed in 1851. Earl Grosvenor subsequently took a lease on the whole of the Reay Forest which in 1866 consisted of Stack, Arkle, Foinaven, Gobernuisgach and Ben Hee. Simultaneously he gradually increased the size of the small house at Lochmore, built between 1856 and 1866 by a Mr Reid, which became his headquarters. As Duke of Westminster he was responsible for many improvements including the building of the stables, offices and laundry at Achfary, and new houses around the estate for stalkers. Hugh Lupus Grosvenor, 1st Duke of Westminster, died on 22 December 1899 aged 74. He was honoured by the tenantry of the district who, as an expression of their deepest respect and gratitude for the employment he had given 'to the comfort of many', erected a wall-mounted tablet to his memory at Achfary. Laxford Bridge, about which more will be said later, lies six miles distant.

Inverauld Lodge, seen here among rhododendrons *c*.1914, lies about half a mile off the Lairg to Lochinver road (the last of the three routes described previously) on the fringe of the Oykel Forest south-west of Lairg. The sender of this postcard wrote: 'We have got up here in the wilds of Sutherlandshire. This is a view of our house. It stands alone surrounded by woods, not a house near. We might as well be out of this world.'

The long finger of Glen Cassley strikes some twelve miles up into the mountains from Strath Oykel, but the actual source of the River Cassley must lie many miles distant, quite lost among a myriad of lochs, lochans and streams in the mountain fastness beyond mighty Ben More Assynt (3,273 feet). The castle in the glen four miles north of Rosehall is a rather striking shooting lodge (incorporating an elaborate tower) completed about 1875. Flowing into the Kyle of Sutherland, the Cassley has a worldwide reputation for salmon fishing, as do the Oykel, Shin and Carron. Indeed, offering both brown and sea-trout in addition, the whole area must be a fisherman's paradise.

The first 'big house' at Rosehall was destroyed by fire in 1817, but Richard Dunning (2nd Lord Ashburton) immediately masterminded a rebuilding programme which saw this rather austere mansion rise from the ashes some five years later. To this end, Moray stone was brought up the River Oykel, and by a canal (constructed specially for the purpose) on the final stage up to the house. He designed and built a variety of other buildings in the locality, but died in 1823 leaving what had become his life's work somewhat incomplete.

In days long gone, pedlars, packmen, tinkers and travellers on foot took the little-frequented route through Strath Oykel, an immense strath which somehow seems all the more dramatic by the approach from Carbisdale Castle to the south. The origins of the Oykel Bridge Hotel (formerly named the Balnagown Arms) go back to 1831 shortly after the construction of the Lochinver road. On a chance call everything may be strangely quiet, nobody immediately evident, tables neatly laid in the dining room, the comfortable lounge deserted – all vaguely reminiscent of the *Marie Celeste*. This is typical of such hotels, where most of the guests will be out trying their luck with rod and line, for this is another well-known fishing hotel.

Above: At Altnacealgach the Ross-shire/Sutherland boundary forms an oddly-shaped wedge up the southern flank of Conival, an outlier of Ben More Assynt. Long ago a dispute took place here between the two counties over the exact line of the boundary, and witnesses were called to give evidence for each. Those from Ross-shire claimed they had never wandered a step off 'their' ground, and neither had they, having first cunningly filled their brogues with Balnagown (Ross-shire) soil! Hence, Altnacealgach – 'the Burn of the Cheat'.
Below: The Lairg to Lochinver mail service makes a stop at Altnacealgach *c.*1911. Old habits die hard; the once important stabling facilities at this former change-house became redundant on the introduction of these vehicles, but the exchange of mail, especially at an inn, remained a convivial occasion.

ELPHIN TO CAPE WRATH

The parish of Assynt, reached from the east by way of Altnacealgach and Ledmore, and through neighbouring Elphin from the south, encompasses the whole area westwards to the coast as far north as Unapool. The Assynt Clearances of 1812 to 1821 were designed to increase the rental income of the Sutherland Estates by consolidating fragmented landholdings in the interior and converting them into a few large and more profitable sheep farms. At the same time, the tenantry were resettled on smaller holdings around the coast between Inverkirkaig and Unapool where official encouragement was given to alternative activities such as fishing and kelp-gathering. While the resettlements were undertaken in the face of strong resistance, and although genuine hardship and poverty resulted for many, they were nonetheless completed largely peaceably (despite a riot at Inchnadamph), and no crofts are known to have been burnt. An attempt to clear Elphin in 1851 was thwarted by determined opposition, with the result that somewhat exceptionally, the original pattern of scattered crofts of traditional appearance still survives here.

Driving south through Assynt towards Ullapool, a motorist stopped to take this photograph on 19 July 1934. Elphin and Cul Mor (2,786 feet) lie ahead. In times of heavy rain or run-off from melting snow, some sections of poorly drained roads such as this might resemble a river bed.

Inchnadamph ('the Stag's Pasturing-place') lies where historic hill tracks converge; long before Lochinver claimed the distinction, the hamlet was pre-eminent in Assynt. In the droving days cattle were gathered around the fertile margin of Loch Assynt before the overland drive south. *Above:* One of the many different faces of Quinag (2,653 feet); the early twentieth century parish church of Assynt (not the first on this site) stands among trees near the loch. The old churchyard contains an ancient MacLeod burial vault while, outside the gate, a memorial commemorates the RAF crew of six who perished when their aircraft crashed on Ben More Assynt in spring 1941. *Centre:* The Old Manse (left, dating from 1821); the post office (foreground) and the much-enlarged hotel. Both photographs *c.*1935.
Right: Over a period of some 250 years, a shelter for travellers and a change-house grew to become an inn, and finally a well-known hotel (pictured here *c.*1910). The signatures of Millicent, Duchess of Sutherland and Osgood MacKenzie of Inverewe appear in the old visitors' book, as do those of two men who aroused the curiosity of the inn's other (mainly angling) guests by spending long hours on the surrounding mountainsides in all weathers, and taking a particular interest in the Traligill Burn, even though they did not fish . . .

On a knoll of Cambrian dolomite above Loch Assynt stands the memorial erected in 1930 to Drs Benjamin Peach and John Horne as an international tribute to their pioneering geological work undertaken around Inchnadamph. Year after year from 1883 they used the inn as a base for their explorations, eventually unravelling the complex geological structure of this area which makes the North-West Highlands unique, and publishing their classic report in 1907. Here are some of the oldest rocks known to Man. Gigantic disturbances in the earth's crust resulting in tremendous thrust-planes have fashioned a geologically chaotic landscape where vastly differing types of rock rest unconformably one with another – features which have long puzzled geologists. The effects, too, of glaciation and erosion by weathering have been significant, and the belief that the last Ice Age extended over 10,000 years, completely burying the Highlands and covering the highest mountains with ice to a maximum depth of perhaps 5,000 feet, is a sobering thought.

The rough road through Assynt, *c*.1920. To have motored in the Highlands in those days was almost something to boast about and, unsurprisingly, early advice to those intent on motoring in Sutherland included the carrying of a *second* spare tyre.

The histories of Ardvreck Castle (a seat of the MacLeods of Assynt dating from *c.*1500) and nearby Calda House are not unconnected. The most noteworthy event concerning the castle occurred in 1650, when the army of Montrose, which espoused the Royalist cause during the Civil War, was routed by forces commanded by General Strachan at the Battle of Carbisdale. 'The Great Marquis' was captured and cast into the dungeon at Ardvreck on 30 April 1650, prior to his execution in Edinburgh three weeks later. The MacKenzies displaced the MacLeods from the castle in 1672, and Calda House was built for Kenneth MacKenzie in 1726. This substantial building, considered unique in the North-West Highlands, is cited as a prototype for other early eighteenth century MacKenzie houses such as Flowerdale and Applecross. Further clan rivalry is thought responsible for the fire which destroyed the house in 1737, since when it has remained a ruin. For those wishing to know more, a comprehensive booklet compiled by Maggie Campbell covering both properties is available locally, the proceeds benefiting these historic sites of Assynt.

Sluice-gates, winding gear and a fish ladder were all components of the dam constructed across the River Inver in 1911, the purpose of which was to control the flow of water thereby creating the best conditions for salmon fishing. Unsurprisingly, perhaps, this control mechanism has not been overwhelmingly popular over the intervening years, having been the cause of much local dissension between the various riparian landlords. The dam has recently been completely refurbished.

There were no roads in any part of Sutherland prior to 1807, and apart from one at Brora the county was entirely lacking in bridges with the result that rivers and streams had to be forded in all weathers. In full spate especially, they were genuine obstacles to travellers (whether on foot or horse), crofters attempting to move their stock, or to those just going about their daily business. This bridge (1821) over the River Inver at Lochinver carries the road to Badidarrach ('Place of the Oaks'); the name inspires a variety of different spellings on local road signs, the Ordnance Survey and elsewhere, so I have taken advice from the indigenous – even indignant – population!

Assynt was purchased by the Sutherland family in 1757 and the settlement at Lochinver was established in 1812 around the bay which provided a natural anchorage and harbour. In this view from the north-east *c*.1906, the road curves around the shore towards the Culag Hotel, the outline of which can be seen (left) backed by woods in the distance. In the foreground on the Badidarrach road is the Free Church (built in 1893). Three separate cottages (when built originally in the mid-nineteenth century), with distinctive chimney stacks set diamondwise, complete the picture.

Angus Mackenzie, a local man born in 1876, worked in Lochinver shops as a lad. In 1900 he opened his first business, the People's Shop, subsequently moving to the Lochinver Stores nearby. This was a substantial business comprising an extensive tailoring enterprise above a general store which incorporated butcher and bakery sections. Note the date-stone 1894 above the porch, the ornate bracket and hanging lamp, the sign 'Ladies and Gents Tailor' and the advertisement for Sutherland Home Industries in the window. This photograph of the staff was taken in the summer of 1913 and shows, *inter alia*, Angus Mackenzie (fifth left) and his sister Peggy (second left).

Lochinver Post Office was opened in 1896 by Willie Wilson, a local shopkeeper. These two scenes are from either side of the First World War. *Above:* The sight of the mail wagonette outside the busy post office always attracted attention. Mail and parcels were handled for Lochinver and the outlying area, while passengers were continually arriving from, or departing for, Lairg. *Below:* In the early days of motoring there was a dearth of facilities in the Highlands, but Lochinver was a welcome exception. Punctures were common, and the tyre stood against the rear of the car (left) might be indicative of a problem experienced on the rough roads. The war memorial (extreme left) is inscribed with 64 names (many from the Seaforth Highlanders) who gave their lives in the 1914–18 conflict. In this close-knit community such a loss must have been grievous; few could have remained untouched, as families that had not directly suffered a loss would have known one that had.

Above: The sheltered anchorage is well illustrated in this photograph of *c.*1905, as is the prominently sited and beautifully proportioned building with lancet windows which has been the Church of Scotland since 1903. Carefully dismantled and shipped to Lochinver for re-erection, the church had previously stood in Nairn for over 50 years before being declared redundant. *Centre:* 'Lochinver, looking to Reading Room and Parish Church', *c.*1903. The need for a communal centre was recognised and addressed under the aegis of the Lochinver Coffee Room Association, formed in 1878. A matron was placed in charge of facilities, which included a library and reading room, and 'food and rest for those respectable citizens requiring these comforts'. Those, at matron's discretion, might 'remain in the reading room over night with light and fire on paying 1/-'. In 1902 a new building was erected at a cost of £168. Beds were purchased for overnight guests, and a variety of evening classes introduced; several newspapers and periodicals were always available. *Right:* Silent sentinel. Suilven – 'the Sugar Loaf' (2,399 feet) – peers above the skyline in this classic Lochinver scene. The Torridonian sandstone mountains of Assynt resting on Lewisian gneiss present weird, even sinister shapes and are among the most unique memorials to geological denudation.

Two scenes on the River Culag, which flows into the south-eastern corner of Lochinver Bay. The bridge, of contemporaneous date with that across the Inver (page 22), gives access to a scenic and adventurous road southwards to Inverkirkaig (home to probably Britain's most remote mainland bookshop), Enard Bay and Badnagyle. Once there, readers of *Old Ways Through Wester Ross* will be in familiar territory: the left fork (east) leads by way of Stac Pollaidh (Stac Polly) and Drumrunie to Ullapool, the right to Achiltibuie and the Summer Isles.

In the ancient Highland tongue Culag means 'a sheltered corner', and according to the reminiscences of Evander MacIver, the Duke of Sutherland's factor in Victorian times, this site was originally developed as a smokehouse for herring in 1775 and known as Lochinver House. The ways of the migratory herring are not fully understood, and fishing for 'the silver darlings' was always a notoriously volatile occupation for which the phrase 'boom and bust' could have been invented. Following the bankruptcy of a previous owner, the Duke acquired the property and in 1845 converted much of the original building into a dwelling-house where his family lived during the summer and autumn months. He also continued the planting of the surrounding Culag woods begun by a previous owner. This house was subsequently gutted by fire, but the restoration and enlargement of 1873 created 'a gentleman's residence'. In this form it was let to Mr MacBrayne (of shipping fame) at a rental of £500 per annum for several years before opening as the Culag Hotel in 1880. MacIver described the Culag as 'one of the most comfortable and well-kept hotels in the west of Scotland, greatly frequented by anglers and tourists'.

M. J. B. Baddeley's *Thorough Guide* of 1885 provides an intriguing commentary on the growth and popularity of Lochinver over the previous twelve years, while also criticising the failure to increase accommodation to match demand. The *Guide* makes this observation on the journey from Lairg: 'it is strange how little in proportion the public means of access to Lochinver has increased during the same period. The 50 miles between Lochinver and Lairg have been for many years traversed daily by two 'machines' – one in each direction – whereof the smaller is a one-horse gig with accommodation for the driver, the mails and three passengers, and the other (facetiously called the 'big' cart), a two-horse vehicle with two cross seats besides the driver's and a carrying capacity in reality for six passengers and a small quantity of luggage, but in practice for as many as can sit, stand, or hang on. This wants seeing to.' It adds that 'the Culag is well and energetically managed and, considering its accommodation [for 60 guests] the charge of 13/6d a day, including attendance, can hardly be thought anything but reasonable'.

Since 1880 much has changed. A serious fire, substantial development within the former walled garden, compounded by the expansion of the fishing port on adjoining land reclaimed from the sea ten years ago, have all irrevocably changed 'the sheltered corner', seen here *c.*1907.

These two views show some of the many changes which have been made both to the Culag Hotel and within the walled garden at the rear. *Top:* Stand on the ornamental stone staircase today and look in the direction of the unknown cameraman who composed this photograph some 90 years ago and the scene has changed beyond recognition. The view is no longer of plants, flowers and vegetables immaculately tended by the gardeners of long ago, but of a housing development completed in the 1990s. *Below:* Where garden paths intersected there was once a magnificent whalebone arch. Adjacent to the former entrance to the walled garden is a range of buildings (one of which bears a date-stone of 1872) once occupied by domestic, gardening and estate staff. (Photograph reproduced here by kind permission of Nicholas Gorton.)

The chauffeur has brought this Paisley-built Arrol Johnston car around to the hotel entrance, and the departing visitors are aboard, *c*.1906. Hector MacKenzie, the hotel 'boots' (or porter) stands on the steps (left). Note the twisted rope moulding around the entrance porch; such ornamentation was not unusual on the more noteworthy Highland properties in Victorian times.

The tragedies of the 1929 Culag Hotel fire were the destruction of a distinctive building which had represented the most enduring symbol of Lochinver, and the death of two guests who were trapped on the main staircase and engulfed in flames. In the early hours of 1 January 1929 the alarm was raised as fire rapidly took hold of the building, which contained a wealth of panelling, wooden floors and estate-made joinery. Able-bodied men turned out, and local police constable Donnie MacBain (pictured here) telegraphed frantically for assistance with the message CULAG BLAZING SEND URGENT ASSISTANCE. The night sky was lit up by the intensity of the blaze, and word spread quickly around the locality. Hogmanay was being celebrated and many who were abroad first-footing that night walked into Lochinver to witness the scene for themselves with shock and utter disbelief.

The ruins remained until 1932 when Mr Ronald Vestey purchased the Assynt Estate, including the shell of the hotel. He commenced the task of rebuilding, and the hotel eventually reopened on the outbreak of the Second World War in 1939. Since the reconstruction there have been many reported sightings of a couple, attired in evening dress, descending the main staircase in the early hours. They reach the final flight of stairs, but never the ground floor, and just fade away into the darkness . . . (Photograph reproduced here by kind permission of Nicholas Gorton.)

Visitors not travelling from Lairg by one of the two 'machines' might well have arrived by either the SS *Claymore* or SS *Clansman* which operated together on the Glasgow–Stornoway route. Each called fortnightly on their outward voyage, but did not call at Lochinver on the return journey, thus ensuring an enforced and frequently unwanted visit to Stornoway. Such vessels sustained small and often remote communities; all manner of goods arrived at the Culag pier to be unloaded and delivered by horse and cart over a wide area. Alternatively, those sufficiently well-heeled and possessing the luxury of a steam yacht might avoid tedious travel over generally poor roads by making good use of safe anchorages, as here at Lochinver. Useful, too, for visiting and impressing one's titled estate-owning associates. However, expensive to operate and crew, steam yachts fell out of favour following the Great War; their golden age had passed.

Sutherland and fishing (whether in the myriad of inland lochs or, as here, in coastal waters) go hand-in-hand. Cod, haddock, ling, pollack and wrasse all provide sport for the sea angler. 'Lochinver annual visitor, his butler and boatman' dates from *c.*1904.

Murdo Kerr was a colourful local character who made his living fishing with his small boat (shown in the previous picture). A noted and certainly much-photographed fisherman, he was the first to provide sea angling trips for visitors. Here he is proudly displaying a 7 lb lobster and 141 lb skate caught on rod and line *c.*1904.

Throughout history the profitability of commercial fishing has been wildly erratic, but nonetheless the scale of the industry has come a long way from the handful of small boats shown at the pier on page 27. At that time activity was confined to line-fishing augmented by the seasonal pursuit of the herring, but as the twentieth century progressed and living standards improved, there was increasing demand for high-quality fish, especially from top London hotels and restaurants. Larger and more powerful boats were natural consequences. Consignments bound for Billingsgate and elsewhere were suitably packed in locally made fish-boxes and ice, and put aboard the bus for Invershin Station and the overnight rail journey south. The coastal waters around Assynt became an early attraction for continental klondykers whose capacity for local fish seemed insatiable. Lochinver also became a home base for Scottish east coast boats.

A continual policy of port facility enhancement culminated in the massive development completed in 1992 which should have ensured the survival of Lochinver as a leading white fish and shellfish port. However, aspects of EU fishing policy – quotas, decommissioning of boats, stocks and conservation matters – have resulted in more exotic and unusual varieties of fish being sought in more distant fishing grounds, especially from Kinlochbervie to the north. As I write, there are unusually no fish auctions being conducted at Lochinver as catches are landed pre-sold, resulting in these most modern of port facilities being under-utilised. The industry is in constant turmoil but, for me, there has been no more heart-warming sight than that of the trawlers safely returning to port one by one with their catches on the evening tide having suffered a buffeting on the storm-tossed waters of the Minch.

ACHMELVICH BAY NEAR LOCHINVER, SUTHERLAND

CLACKTOLL, Near STOER, SUTHERLAND.

CLACHTOLL AND STOER FROM THE SOUTH

The road around the coastal margin between Lochinver and Unapool is a gem and one to savour; a short diversion leads to a bay of white sand at Achmelvich, quite deserted in this picture from earlier days. These North Assynt lands were resettled following the Clearances referred to earlier.

Norman MacLeod was born in 1780 at nearby Clachtoll. What later became his controversial, outspoken, even rebellious attitudes were shaped by the injustices of the Clearances and his disillusionment with the Established Church from which he parted company. By 1815 he had successfully completed his studies for the Ministry and was preaching his own particular brand of fiery evangelism which attracted a band of followers known as 'Normanites', thereby, in a sense, anticipating the Disruption of 1843. In 1817 MacLeod and the Normanites sailed from Loch Broom on the *Frances Ann* to settle in Pictou, Nova Scotia – in fact only the first stage of an epic journey which was to take them to Cape Breton, Australia and finally to Waipu (North Island, New Zealand) where the colony of some 800 prospered. MacLeod died there in 1866 where a memorial commemorates these early Scottish settlers; another 128 years were to pass before a rough-hewn block of Assynt marble was erected on the north shore of Clachtoll Bay in memory of this leader of men.

By a twist of fate the 21,000 acre North Assynt Estate (which includes Clachtoll) was the subject of a landmark community buyout in 1992, the first major experiment in community land ownership in the Highlands. 'Why would we want to buy it back?' commented one, 'we already own it'. Somehow, I feel, the Reverend Norman MacLeod would have liked that!

In this 1930s photograph the Thomas Telford designed 'Parliamentary' church at Stoer is not only roofed, but also displays a bellcote. This has since been replaced by a cross, the bellcote having been removed and remounted on a low extension of the former manse, Stoer House (extreme right), while the church is now a mere shell and open to the sky. The adjacent Stoer peninsula is the most westerly part of Sutherland, and some claim that local peats are the finest in the county. The lighthouse on the headland was built in 1870 by the Stevenson brothers (and made automatic in 1976); the Old Man of Stoer, an isolated sea stack, stands 200 feet high near the Point. At Culkein slipway, once a point of entry for seaborne goods into the district, mouldering buildings testify to a former importance.

There may be more than a grain of truth in the saying that a croft is 'a small plot of land surrounded by legislation'. However, this traditional crofting scene – thatched byres, and stooks drying in the wind in view of the sea at Clashnessie – has a timeless quality which encapsulates the very essence of the west.

An unknown photographer has provided us with a series of glimpses. The skilfully engineered narrow road around the cliffs is supported by deep stone embankments descending sheer to the sea; one can only guess what lies around the blind corner. In the distance, regiments of stooks are drawn up in the fields almost in battle formation. The sands at Clashnessie Bay are more extensive than the photograph reveals – and are usually deserted; another of Assynt's best-kept secrets. Definitely a road to linger along.

Over the hill, immediately behind Oldany House (right) and Lodge, lies Oldany Island with its ancient burial ground. Island burials have a long tradition and were often made where the depth of soil was insufficient for local interments, and to avoid the predations of wolves. Historically, too, suicides have been set apart. This postcard, issued through Angus Mackenzie's 'People's Shop' in Lochinver, dates from 1904.

William Ross was born in Glenleraig in 1884. Both postcards bear the imprint of 'W. Ross, Postcard Publisher, Drumbeg', and were sold over the counter some time before the First World War at the store which displays his name. The purchaser, a regular guest at the hotel, wrote a note on the back of each before posting them in an envelope, for neither are postally used. *Top:* 'This is our principal shop, and does a bigger trade than you would suppose from its appearance – about £800 per year turnover, or more perhaps. The girl in the door is saleswoman and bookkeeper.' *Above:* 'A great many anglers from the south put up here in the season. I stayed here for three months when I came here first. It is a Temperance Hotel; we have no dram shop here at all.'

Top: In the bay, a scattering of low islands; along the line of the narrow road 'twixt loch and sea, the few buildings include (left to right) the Drumbeg stores and hotel (centre), the school (built 1878 and now closed), and the small library (nearest the road intersection) donated in 1909 by Millicent, Duchess of Sutherland. This is now the Associated Presbyterian Church of Scotland. Prior to the First World War the road degenerated here to a mere track by which remote and isolated Ardvar was reached. Those who shunned the more conventional Lochinver to Kylesku route (via Skiag Bridge) could take an 'occasional' ferry across the exposed waters of Eddrachillis Bay to Badcall, continuing their journey overland to Scourie. The Drumbeg ferryman charged 10/- for the six-mile row ('uncomfortable in anything but really good weather'), and provided accommodation for those whose crossing might be delayed by unfavourable conditions. Some ruins of his house remain near the shore. *Below:* By 1915 the road, extended eastwards by this time from Drumbeg to Kylesku, was described as 'very hilly and still very rough, although a new and most interesting through road from Lochinver to Kylesku'. This development spelt the death-knell for the Drumbeg ferry. Nedd, on the new section, is dominated by the dark mass of Quinag, *c.*1935.

The bridge at Glenleraig *c.*1912. Sharp ascents and descents characterise this severe road which caused difficulties for one motorist in July 1933: 'Trouble beset us in the shadow of the Quinag for the car and van stuck on a perpendicular piece of road, and the road being of such a soft nature, the wheels would not grip'. After trying again and again they gave up and went for help finding 'three stalwart men who we harnessed to the car, and then having strewn the road with heather we all did our best and up the old car and van went like a bird. Indeed, they're strong men the West Highlanders, and so dour, they didn't even register pleasure at a reward of a £1 note each; at a length we reached Kylesku!'

A footpath by way of Gleann Leireag and the bealach leads under mighty Quinag to Loch Assynt Lodge, conspicuously sited near the Lochinver to Skiag Bridge road.

Beyond the old sheep farm by Loch Ardvar, the winding road alongside Loch Cairnbawn to Unapool and Kylesku passes through sheltered birch woods, the remnants of the once extensive north-western forest. Lochs Cairnbawn, Glendhu and Glencoul converge at Kylesku to form an immense fjord, the product of a distant Ice Age. From time immemorial this major obstacle to north/south travel up the west coast was overcome by the operation of a small ferry, but in 1984 a spectacular bridge was built in this wild place.

Kylesku has an awesome setting. The huge surrounding panorama is dominated by majestic mountains rising from remote fastnesses which form some of the most inaccessible areas of Britain. The complex geology of the north-west is clearly seen on the mountainside across Loch Glencoul, which provides the best example of a thrust fault in the British Isles, while at the head of the loch Britain's highest waterfall, Eas Coul Aulin, with a drop of over 650 feet, is four times the height of Niagara. The Kylesku narrows are a very ancient crossing-place, and a ferry had been in operation since the seventeenth century or earlier. In the droving days, the black cattle of North-West Sutherland were swum across on their way to the trysts at Muir of Ord and Falkirk. The photographer taking the picture on the right nearly a century ago was facing a building dating largely from 1890, but long before then there had been a small inn here, and even further back in time just the ferryman's wee house. Small Highland ferries have now passed into history, including that at Kylesku. The crossing here took barely five minutes, but provided a vital link for the movement of vehicles, passengers, animals and supplies; the alternative was a diversion of nearly 100 miles via Lairg and Laxford Bridge to reach the jetty opposite at Kylestrome. In the hotel bar, John Hugh Ross spoke of Kylesku days long ago – of the Vikings and Spanish graves and of herring shoals trapped in the lochs. John was one of nine ferrymen at the time the ferry service was withdrawn in 1984. 'The demise of the ferry was a disaster', he recalled, 'statistics showed that nine people lost their jobs, but it was nine *families* that were affected'.

A.2303. AT KYLE SKU FERRY, SUTHERLAND.

In days past, the realisation that your planned motoring route would necessarily include the transport of the car over water requiring the services of a Highland ferry might justifiably have engendered a feeling of mild anxiety. There was the excitement of actually reaching the ferry point, and only then would your place in the likely queue become apparent. A glance at the opposite shore would indicate how many vehicles were waiting to cross in the reverse direction, and the waiting time could then be gauged. Time enough, perhaps, for some refreshment at the hotel. Other factors, too, could cause delay: at some ferries arrival at lunchtime might find the ferryman taking a break. Sudden deterioration in weather conditions could lead to delayed or cancelled sailings resulting in the inability to reach an intended destination by nightfall, and the need for hasty rearrangement of accommodation. At Kylesku in the 1960s, if bad weather prevented a sailing, a red flag was flown at the south pier; if low tides caused a temporary stoppage, a yellow flag was flown. Further difficulties facing the motorist included the possibility of an awkward, angled entry onto the ferry ramp, or wheelspin as tyres failed to grip the smooth cobbles on the slipway which were often wet and/or covered with seaweed. Memorable days!

A2372 KYLE-SKU FERRY, SUTHERLAND.

Above: Safely across at Kylestrome: the view over the narrows towards Kylesku, and, *left*, a motorcyclist awaits the ferry in 1937. At one time a fee of 6/- was payable for a car up to 10 h.p., but on taking over the ferry in 1948 Sutherland County Council operated the service free of charge for many years on the basis that the crossing was technically an extension of the road either side of the loch where there was no realistic alternative for travellers.

Beyond Kylestrome Lodge (Grosvenor Estates) the next leg of the northbound journey to Scourie was over a corkscrew-like road, whose execrable surface was described by one writer in 1953 as resembling 'a cart-track and full of potholes', despite having an official 'A' classification. By 1958 the surface had been tarred; on our first visit a few years later, the RAC described the route as 'narrow with steep gradients and numerous blind corners'. Exactly so; the eleven miles to Scourie then took one hour to negotiate. Today's motorists, driving over the graceful bridge at Kylesku and by a fine road north, can have no comprehension of how their counterparts had to cope 40 years earlier.

The old manse of Eddrachillis (foreground) overlooks Badcall Bay (an arm of Eddrachillis Bay) and the fishing station by the shore: both date from the 1830s. The latter, a two-storied building complete with living accommodation and an ice house when built, was established as a salmon processing station and is seen here *c.*1935. *Below:* In 1724 the parish of Durness was divided into three: Tongue, Durness and Eddrachillis. Previously the area between Tongue and Kylesku had formed one huge parish whose religious needs had been administered by just one clergyman. While the former manse is now an hotel, the parish church of Eddrachillis (*c.*1728) became a private residence about 30 years ago. Many have found enchantment in the sublime seascape of green islands in the bay where sunsets can be overwhelmingly stunning. Up until the First World War, in the northern corner of Badcall Bay, the rowing-boat ferry from Drumbeg landed travellers for Scourie, three miles distant. Similarly, Scourie folk used the ferry to attend the twice-yearly series of services which began on a Thursday and concluded the following Monday during 'the Communion Season' at Drumbeg.

Top: North of Kylesku, the construction of the more direct present-day highway has resulted in the stranding of significant loops of the former road at Duartmore and Duartbeg. At Scourie, too, a bypass now sweeps around the croftland replacing the original narrow approach to the village shown here in the 1930s. The rugged background of Lewisian gneiss contrasts sharply with the gentle, orderly pattern of dry-stane dykes and fields under cultivation. *Above:* At the distant intersection of the curving road through the village stands the Scourie Hotel with its carefully tended and productive gardens. Scourie House lies behind, among trees; to the left, a glimpse of the bay – sandy, sheltered and safe – and the jetty. In the late 1920s an unknown photographer captured the essentials of the village in this well-composed picture.

The heart of Scourie *c*.1900. Nineteenth century buildings, some crow-stepped, lie in the lee of the hills.

In the village.

Scourie Beach, *c*.1900. The bay offers fishing, sea-bathing and interesting rock pools at low tide.

Occupying the site of the old fortified house of the Mackays of Scourie, part of the Scourie Hotel dates back over two centuries, and hospitality has been available to travellers since at least 1823. As long ago as 1885, when there was a dearth of accommodation in the remote north-west and touring was very much an adventure, the hotel was described as 'good and comfortable'. While outwardly the frontage (seen here in late Victorian times) has changed significantly, the hotel continues to cater chiefly for anglers, ornithologists and those wishing to explore this unique area.

During the last two decades of Queen Victoria's reign, Scourie must have seemed 'the very back of beyond'. The only public conveyance, the mail-cart, took 7 ¾ hours to cover the 44 mile journey to Lairg (passengers 12/-), while the 26 miles to Durness took 3 ½ hours (fare 6/-). The new age of motoring brought substantial benefits, reducing the Lairg run by 2 ⅕ hours by 1915. However, this Albion wagonette of *c.*1906 at Scourie Post Office still lacked any protection from the elements for passengers. Local information suggests that the picture dates from 1912; the driver is Archie Moffat of Scourie, while Angus MacKenzie (standing) had formerly driven horse-drawn coaches for the Sutherland Coaching Company. The outline of Scourie House is visible in the background.

Scourie House, an M-gabled mansion complete with crow-steps and chimney stacks set diamondwise, dates from the 1840s. The house was originally built for the Sutherland Estates factor, Evander MacIver, who held this important position for about 50 years from 1846 and whose reminiscences, *Memoirs of a Highland Gentleman*, provided a glimpse of the early history around 'the sheltered corner' at Lochinver.

From the Isles of Scilly in the south to northernmost Sutherland, the climate of our western seaboard is influenced by the warm waters originating in the Gulf of Mexico which flow across the Atlantic Ocean and around the northern coasts of the British Isles. The moderating effects of the Gulf Stream, more correctly known as the North Atlantic Drift, produce milder, more humid weather patterns enabling plants, shrubs and trees to flourish in locations where they would never otherwise do so. At 58° N, Scourie lies on a more northerly latitude than either Labrador or Moscow. While this greenhouse at Scourie House may have vanished, the palm trees planted about 1870 and generated from New Zealand seed still flourish, and can claim to be not merely the most northerly *established* palm trees in the British Isles, but also in the world!

R.2222. THE STACK OF HANDA ISLAND, SCOURIE, SUTHERLAND.

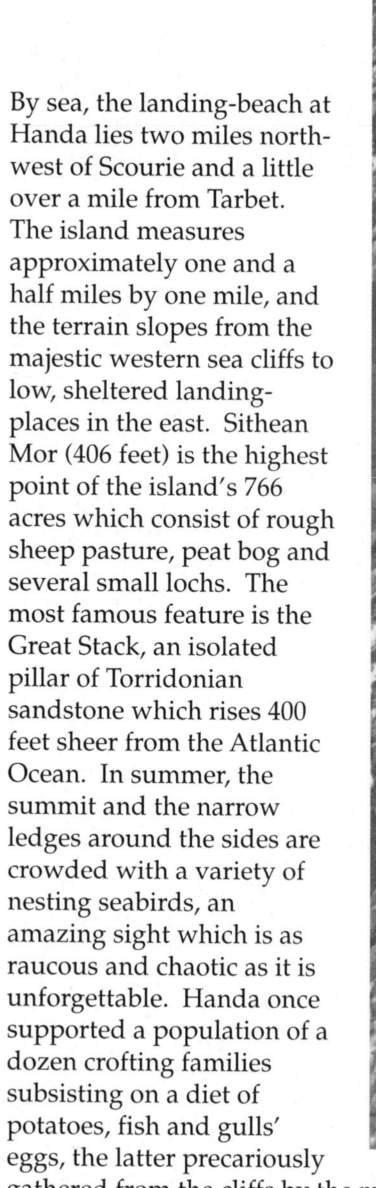

By sea, the landing-beach at Handa lies two miles north-west of Scourie and a little over a mile from Tarbet. The island measures approximately one and a half miles by one mile, and the terrain slopes from the majestic western sea cliffs to low, sheltered landing-places in the east. Sithean Mor (406 feet) is the highest point of the island's 766 acres which consist of rough sheep pasture, peat bog and several small lochs. The most famous feature is the Great Stack, an isolated pillar of Torridonian sandstone which rises 400 feet sheer from the Atlantic Ocean. In summer, the summit and the narrow ledges around the sides are crowded with a variety of nesting seabirds, an amazing sight which is as raucous and chaotic as it is unforgettable. Handa once supported a population of a dozen crofting families subsisting on a diet of potatoes, fish and gulls' eggs, the latter precariously gathered from the cliffs by the most daring of the island cragsmen. Bird feathers were sold or bartered on the mainland in return for wool. The oldest widow was recognised as the Queen of Handa on both the island and the mainland, and was the final arbiter in cases of dispute. Not unlike St Kilda, a 'parliament' or council of men met daily to discuss island business. However, in 1848 the devastating effects of the potato famine resulted in the emigration of the 60 islanders to America, and although the folk are long gone, the outlines of some of their ruined crofts remain a moving testament to the existence of a community once both small and vibrant, but which is now largely forgotten. Today, Handa is home only to sheep and 100,000 seabirds. The island was established as an important bird reserve by the Royal Society for the Protection of Birds by agreement with the proprietors in 1962, but since 1991 the site has been administered by the Scottish Wildlife Trust. The original survey undertaken by the RSPB in 1962 listed a host of differing species of breeding birds, including an estimated 26,000–30,000 pairs of guillemot, with the other most prevalent species – kittiwake, razorbill and fulmar – numbering 7,000, 6,000 and 2,000 pairs respectively.

Right: At the head of Loch Laxford ('The Salmon Loch'), the solitary road junction at Laxford Bridge is prominently marked on maps. The bridge, built in the 1830s, carries the road north, while in the distance the way to Lairg curves through a tremendous glen between Ben Arkle (centre) and Ben Stack in the Reay Forest. So impressed was he by this section of the journey that the late H. V. Morton wrote: 'If I could show a stranger just one glimpse of Highland scenery, this is the one I would choose for him'.

Centre: Seen here *c.*1908, the Rhiconich Hotel stood at the head of Loch Inchard, a loch known to the Vikings as *Engi-fjord* ('Meadow Loch'). Subsequently the hotel was destroyed by fire, and a small police station partially occupies the site today. Manned by just one officer who patrols the area between Kylesku and Laid, this is reputedly the most extensive beat in Britain. Despite the caption, Rhiconich lies over 40 miles from Lairg and is in fact situated a few miles north of Laxford Bridge.

Below: The Kinlochbervie to Durness mail coach at the Rhiconich Hotel *c.*1906. (Photograph reproduced here by kind permission of Peter Burr.)

Until the early nineteenth century, the only 'roads' in North-West Sutherland were a network of drovers' routes. The potato blight which destroyed crops in successive years between 1845 and 1848 brought widespread deprivation and famine to the Highlands and Islands, leaving many communities destitute amid the most dreadful scenes of degradation and poverty. To alleviate the suffering, the Duke of Sutherland paid local people – both men and women – to build a road between Rhiconich and Sheigra on the coast, thereby enabling them to purchase food for their families (hence the name 'destitution roads'). By such efforts the numerous small crofting settlements along the northern coast of Loch Inchard either side of Kinlochbervie (seen here *c.*1910) became more effectively linked to the outside world. In the 1960s the more hazardous features of this road were eliminated upon the designation of Kinlochbervie as a 'specified port'. Piped water was laid on in 1952; electricity followed four years later. *Below:* Kinlochbervie Post Office *c.*1906.

Right: The pictorial history of this building can be traced through a sequence of three photographs. Kinlochbervie House was a two-storied building of traditional nineteenth century style with crow-stepped gables. Situated in an elevated position about 200 yards from the sea, the view from the porch looked directly to what in the 1920s was the tiny fishing harbour of Loch Clash.

Centre: Subsequently suitably enlarged and adapted, the house became the much-loved Garbet Hotel, a premier fishing hotel in the north-west and the hub of the Kinlochbervie Estate which extended over some 50 square miles. Interestingly enough this hotel – to which I referred in my foreword – is one of only three designated as such on the title page map.

Below: The estate, which included a farm, also owned and had sporting rights over 17,000 acres, possessing seventeen lochs of which three held salmon and sea trout, and the remainder brown trout. Additionally, the Garbet was able to provide fishing on another 30 lochs on the adjoining estate, including the famous sea trout loch, Loch Stack. A fisherman's paradise, indeed! Described by one guest as 'a rabbit warren', the final photograph shows the hotel before fire swept through the building in the early hours of 13 August 1965. A fire appliance despatched from Tain in Ross-shire took three and a half hours to reach Kinlochbervie over the narrow roads, but by then the building had become a smouldering ruin, quite beyond rescue. The proprietor, Mrs L. M. Neilson, immediately set about the sad task of reconstruction, and the architecturally very different building which arose on the site and opened for business on 31 May 1966 still stands today.

Above: This church is one of a number built to the standard design of engineer Thomas Telford in 1829 following the Act for Building Additional Places of Worship in the Highlands and Islands of Scotland (1823). Consequently, such churches and their manses are often referred to as 'Parliamentary Plan' buildings. Shown *c.*1906 within a walled plot of land, the former Church of Scotland parish church later became the Free Presbyterian Church. *Below:* To complicate matters still further, the United Free Church and manse pictured here, also *c.*1906, have now become Church of Scotland; these buildings have new neighbours as the modern local primary and high schools have been built nearby in, appropriately enough, Manse Road.

Above: Old buildings, stores and tarred sheds line the narrow road to Loch Clash pier, *c*.1930. *Below:* The two-masted SS *Clansman* (1870–1909) was designed specifically for the arduous Glasgow to Stornoway route which she worked in tandem with the *Claymore* for many years. Regarded as a beauty of her day, a clipper bow, bowsprit and figurehead, accompanied by ornamental carving fore-and-aft, were unusual embellishments. Electric lighting was installed in 1904. Seen leaving Loch Clash some time prior to 1908, her gross weight of 600 tons and overall length of 211 feet necessitated the building of the first pier of substance here (foreground).

These two photographs from the 1930s give an indication of the modest level of activity during those years. In 1951 fresh impetus was injected following the acquisition of local interests, both here and at Rhiconich, by the Second Duke of Westminster. Subsequently, Loch Clash has lost out to the more sheltered Loch Bervie, with the result that the centre of operations has shifted progressively to up-to-date facilities established there. Current fishing policy imposed from Brussels has dictated reduced reliance on traditional catches of white fish in favour of other species. Large trawlers now go much further afield to fish waters up to a mile deep off the edge of the continental shelf around the Rockall Trough in order to exploit more unusual species. These find ready sale on the continent but are largely unfamiliar to us: rabbit fish, blue ling, black scabbard fish, greater silver smelts, red fish ('Norway haddock') and deep water skate. Kinlochbervie continues to make news, however. Two years ago the trawler *Enterprise II*, operating off Rockall, pulled from the sea an eight foot long halibut weighing twenty stone and thought to be 35 years old (generally halibut average between 6–12 lbs).

Chief among the few small crofting settlements on the coast beyond Kinlochbervie is Oldshore More, where some of those evicted during the Strathnaver Clearances of 1814 and 1819 were resettled. Sparsely populated today, the area was once well-cultivated, wooded and relatively populous. A narrow track continues to the formerly important old pier at nearby Droman before petering out at Sheigra. Study this picture long enough, and I feel sure you will see eventually over the sea in the far west the legendary Celtic paradise of Tir nan Og ('Land of the Ever Young').

Sandwood Bay is the most north-westerly beach in mainland Britain where waves which have rolled 3,000 miles across the North Atlantic Ocean find landfall on a remote shore of pure sand. Said to be awesome in a hurricane, the bay is guarded on the south side by an isolated sea stack, Am Buachaille ('The Herdsman'), while six miles to the north across the bogs and peat hags of the moors of the Parph lies Cape Wrath and the lighthouse. From Viking times, many ships have gone to their grave along this wild coast. At Sandwood there is also a ruined cottage and an inland loch. Much has been written of ghostly happenings and unexplained experiences in the district – especially of Sandy Gunn's celebrated and much-reported encounter with a mermaid on 5 January 1900. Author and photographer G. Douglas Bolton wrote aptly of 'a feeling that strange and curious things have happened and would happen again if you stayed long enough'. What is it about Sandwood? Best not go alone, perhaps . . .

KEOLDALE HOTEL, DURNESS

In the twelve miles between Rhiconich and Keoldale (on the Kyle of Durness), Foinaven (2,980 feet) and Cranstackie (2,630 feet) are pre-eminent mountains. Halfway along the route by the roadside at Carbreck is Lawson's Well, a delightful memorial to the construction of this 1830s road which was erected by the surveyor Peter Lawson 'as a mark of gratitude and respect to the inhabitants of Durness and Eddrachillis for their hospitality while projecting this road'.

The two-storied house at Keoldale (also 1830s), with its crow-stepped gables and diamondwise chimney stacks, has a history of occupation by the factors of Balnakeil on behalf of the Lords of Reay. Certainly up to 1915 at least the property was described as 'the farm and offices at Keoldale'. The circular walled garden (contained within a larger overall enclosure) is believed to be unique in the north-west.

KEOLDALE HOTEL, DURNESS.

A.2271. THE CAPE WRATH HOTEL AND KYLE OF DURNESS, SUTHERLAND

The 1920s photographs above show the transition of the former factor's house to the Keoldale Hotel, while a later change of name to the Cape Wrath Hotel was accompanied by considerable enlargement to the old house, together with the addition of extra outbuildings. Seen over the kyle, the road across the Parph to Cape Wrath is reached by the small Keoldale ferry.

Even at high water there is little depth in the upper reaches of the Kyle of Durness (half a mile wide at the ferry point), and at low tide as the waters recede seawards, acres of glistening sand are revealed. During the closing years of Queen Victoria's reign information provided to travellers included: 'Carriages are taken across the ferry at any time except two or three hours at low tide. Horses have to be taken about four miles around, and can only cross at low tide. No conveyances are to be had on the west side of the ferry.' The conveyance of carriages may surprise some, but a picture in *Last Ferry to Skye* of a tinker's caravan aboard a rowing boat illustrates how such matters were accomplished. These photographs show a party en route for Cape Wrath on 18 July 1934, and the ferryman's boats at his slipway in the 1920s. At Keoldale, as I well remember, the waving of a handkerchief in the direction of the ferry-house was then enough to bring the ferryman across the kyle to take you 'Cape side'.

THE KYLE OF DURNESS FROM THE WINDING ROAD TO CAPE WRATH, SUTHERLAND. A.2273

Safely across the kyle, Keoldale is seen from above the ferry-house; Cape Wrath lighthouse lies twelve miles distant over a narrow, tortuous road. The west side was once home to several tiny communities – at Achiemore (where in the 1930s ten children attended school), Diall, Inshore and Kervaig – a scattered population of some three dozen, excluding the lighthouse keepers. The men were shepherds for the most part; now only ruined dwellings serve as poignant reminders of past habitation.

In those days, the Northern Lighthouse Board lorry collected provisions and essentials brought across by ferry, and distributed them to cottages along the route back to the lighthouse. Walkers might be lucky enough to get a lift. Motors were a rarity, although the first car had reached the Cape in 1928. The ford at Diall was always tricky and two people are closely observing this vehicle's progress in midstream.

CROSSING THE FORD ON THE ROAD TO CAPE WRATH, SUTHERLAND. A.2270

A.2274 THE NARROW BRIDGE ON THE ROAD TO CAPE WRATH, SUTHERLAND

While some hiked the weary miles to the Cape, others hired cycles from the ferry-house (10/- in 1915, 'wire the night before'). Opposite Loch Inshore, tourists could once obtain a glass of milk at a cottage, the last habitation directly on the lighthouse road. Very welcome, no doubt! Cape Wrath is the most north-westerly point of mainland Britain, and no matter how one has reached here there is a sense of achievement as, at last, the lighthouse comes into view.

CAPE WRATH, SUTHERLAND.

Sutherland, a seemingly strange name for one of Britain's two most northerly mainland counties, derives from *Sudhr-land* ('The South Land'), a name bestowed by the Norsemen who occupied and ruled North-West Scotland between the eighth and thirteenth centuries. Originating from the viks and fjords of western and southern Norway, these Creekmen or Vikings were consummate boat builders and intrepid seafarers. Their sagas are full of poetry. To them, the sky was the 'Wind Weaver', rain was the 'Tears of the Cloud', and the sea was the 'Glittering Home'. They were both raiders and traders, and as they swept along the 'sea road' from Norway to Ireland via Shetland and Orkney, they left in their wake evidence of their occupation in the many place-names which survive to this day. Spread before me as I write are sheets nine and ten of the Ordnance Survey One-Inch map series covering North-West Sutherland, and there is a noticeable scattering of names and appendages such as: bol, cleit, dal, geo, gil, ness, sgeir, stac and vik – all of which are Viking. As their long ships came under the 900 foot high cliffs of Clò Mòr, the loftiest in mainland Britain, they named the uttermost cliff of Sutherland *Hvarf* – 'the Turning Point'. Never was a name more apt, for it was at Cape Wrath that these sea-reivers from Scandinavia turned southwards towards sunnier seas, the Hebrides, the Isle of Man and Ireland, leaving behind the cold northern latitudes and the tempestuous seas of the Pictland (or Pentland) Firth. Centuries of conflict came to a head during the reign of Alexander III. Readied for a decisive strike and accompanied by the largest fleet ever to have left Norway, the Norse King Haco (or Haakon) set sail from Bergen, his course bringing him around 'the Turning Point' and down the western seaboard. He intended to settle finally the disputed claims over the Hebrides, but was comprehensively outmanoeuvred and beaten by the Scots at the Battle of Largs in 1263. As a result the Hebrides passed to the Crown of Scotland, and Haco's defeat also marked the beginning of the end of Norse colonisation in the north-west.

From time immemorial ships have foundered around this treacherous coast. Recently, a shipwreck believed to be that of a Spanish galleon from the Great Armada of 1588 has been located off Kinlochbervie and is currently under evaluation. In 1802, alarmed by a series of losses, shipping interests demanded action and that a light be placed on the Cape. The cliffs range between 370 and 523 feet in height, and in this spectacular position the renowned engineer and lighthouse designer, Robert Stevenson (1772–1850), built his light. John Gibb of Aberdeen was contracted to build the tower (of dressed stone), while the associated buildings – keepers' accommodation, stores and walled enclosure – were constructed of blocks of granite quarried at Clash

Carnoch, close at hand. Working conditions must have been wretched on this exposed site overlooking the turbulent Atlantic Ocean. The total cost was £14,000. First lit in 1828, the light is visible for 27 miles, giving one revolution every minute and originally showing white and red alternately. The construction of a jetty in a small cove one mile east of the lighthouse as the crow flies enabled stores to be landed by the Northern Lighthouse Board tender.

The primary duties of the complement of three keepers centred around the light, foghorn and radio beacon, but also extended to all routine maintenance and keeping the station spick and span. In the very early days potatoes, turnips and cabbages were successfully grown within the walled enclosure, and a few goats and cows enabled home-made butter and cheese to be produced. Visitors who had made the journey across the Parph needed to be 'shown around', and in June 1966 we used the newly introduced minibus service (seen below). Eighty-one steps took us up to the lamp room and gallery where, with one of the keepers, we followed the progress of a trawler around the headland. She flew the flag of the USSR and was packed with radio antennae – perhaps less of a 'trawler' than she seemed. This took place during the Cold War, when lighthouses were given a Ministry of Defence telephone number to report shipping movements of the Communist Bloc countries.

In 1983 the Northern Lighthouse Board disposed of the ferry rights, ferry-house and slipway at the Kyle of Durness. Worse was to come. The light at Cape Wrath was made automatic in February 1998, and the keepers were withdrawn. Shortly thereafter, Radio Scotland's moving farewell to the disappearing lighthousemen everywhere, *Will the last man to leave please turn on the light*, paid a respectful tribute to the service. On the programme Kenny Weir, keeper at the Cape, said: 'People think we must be lonely stuck out here, but there are far more lonely people in the heart of London. There is a freedom to the job.' Gone forever, a unique way of life had passed into the pages of history. Haunted only by seabirds, the Atlantic wind and ghosts of the past, the lighthouse remains a memorial to the builders and to those who worked there. Tonight and every night as twilight turns to dusk over the desolate moors of the Parph, an automatic signal will activate the light which has shone out reassuringly since 1828. While outwardly nothing appears to have changed, there is now one important difference. No one is at home.

THE NORTH COAST

Right and centre: This extreme north-westerly area of mainland Britain had long been settled: to the Vikings, Durness had been their 'Deer's Point' (or Cape). Much later, curious and adventurous Victorian and Edwardian travellers may have taken comfort in knowing that an hotel lay at this point on their route – the only one on 50 miles of indifferent road between Rhiconich and Tongue. Solidly built of stone, the Durness Hotel, seen here *c.*1900, incorporated crow-stepped gables and probably dated from the early nineteenth century. The provision of mains water about 1906 did not prevent the building being completely destroyed by fire two years later.

Below: The hotel ruins, *c.*1935. For 50 years following the fire until the shell was demolished, the stark ruins were a constant and tangible reminder of the destruction wrought in 1908. In 1959 the remaining stonework was utilised in an extension for the school, and the empty space created enabled the village centre to be replanned. A car park and village information board now occupy the site.

Durine, Durness *c*.1900. The policy of enforced eviction to make way for sheep was first felt locally about 1820 when Balnakeil and Keoldale were cleared, but the Durine survived intact. The census of 1901 recorded the inhabitants of this scattered and sparsely populated district at just 903 persons. Crofting has traditionally sustained the local economy, but today tourist-related activities, of which the Balnakeil Craft Village is but one example, have become increasingly important. To walk in the footsteps of this man in the Durine today is to appreciate the nature of the changes which have taken place here in the last century.

'Durness: Hotel – none. Comfortable lodgings at Mackay's, Parkhill House; two good bedrooms and sitting-room; plain, clean, good' (M. J. B. Baddeley's *Thorough Guide*, 1915). This family-run hotel still provides hospitality, although on a larger scale than in 1915. Other changes, too, have taken place since this 1930s photograph was taken. R. Mackay & Sons, General Merchants, moved to a new site about twenty years ago to become the Mace supermarket, and the Shell facilities once available for motorists have been replaced by those of BP.

Two buildings of importance lie just above the immense one and a half mile sweep of white sand at Balnakeil – the ruins of the former Durness parish church and Balnakeil House (completed in 1744). The date is deceptive, however, for the house is not the first on this site, as the present structure incorporates parts which are much earlier. A monastic building once stood here to serve the church and became a summer residence of the bishops of Caithness in medieval times. The powerful Clan Mackay has been a force to be reckoned with in the north-west since the thirteenth century, and by the sixteenth century the property had passed to the chiefs of that clan who, as Lords of Reay, had their principal residence at Tongue. Courts were held at Balnakeil, and the condemned were hung at nearby Loch Croispol ('Loch of the Gallows'). There are also interesting agricultural buildings, some ruined.

The burial ground and roofless church at Balnakeil are of great antiquity. The ruins date from 1619 and are believed to stand on the site of a medieval chapel. Even further back in time, an early settlement centred on Balnakeil where St Maelrubha founded a church in 720. The handsome obelisk (centre) is a memorial to the Reay Gaelic Bard, Robert Calder Mackay (1714–1778), better known as Rob Donn (Doun), and was erected 'at the expense of a few of his countrymen, ardent admirers of his native talent and extraordinary genius in 1827'. He was held in high esteem, and tributes are inscribed on the obelisk in Greek, Latin, Gaelic and English. Although illiterate, Donn inherited a rich oral tradition of Gaelic music and culture from his mother. His poetry reflected the social life of his times in songs of the shieling, the harvest, wool-waulking and the drove road. The simple lichened flagstone covering his grave gives the year of his death incorrectly as 1777; if local tradition is to be believed the mason carving the date found the chiselling of a figure eight beyond his capability!

Top: Regular, neatly cultivated strips form patterns on the landscape at Sangomore, *c.*1935.
Above: Taken together these two photographs form a panorama of Sangomore ('the Big Sands') where coastal erosion has long caused concerns. There is not a tree to be seen along this part of the windswept coast which is continually drenched in the spume of the northern seas. In these, the most empty of lands in mainland Britain, one wonders how long the cameraman waited for the solitary horse and cart to appear on the road in order to complete his picture.

Smoo Cave – a natural wonder of this coast – stands at the head of a narrow coastal inlet (geo) formed over the centuries by the pounding action of wind and waves on the cliffs. The cave, too, has been fashioned by erosion as the waters of the Smoo burn have worn away and then cut through the limestone rock. The awesomely wide entrance gives access to three caverns of cathedral-like proportions where, through one of two vertical shafts in the roof, the burn plunges 80 feet into a deep pool below. Archaeological evidence suggests that Smoo has been occupied at various times in history, possibly as early as the Mesolithic period, about 6500 BC. Unsurprisingly, such a strange and eerie setting has inspired tales of the supernatural. Smoo Lodge (on the cliff-top, extreme right), one of the 'big houses' of the north coast, dates from the seventeenth century having been built by an Orkney merchant, Murdo Lowe, whose boats traded from the geo below. He is said to have employed local women to carry bolls of meal weighing 140 lbs up the steep path by the now roofless store to the lodge for the payment of an oaten biscuit.

Sangobeag seascape showing Eilean Hoan (left). Willie Morrison was born at Sangomore in January 1941 during one of the century's most severe winters. Within weeks his parents moved into the family croft at nearby Sangobeag upon the death of his paternal grandfather. Willie has spent a lifetime in journalism, and overleaf he recalls memories of his early childhood on the North Sutherland croft during and after the Second World War.

'The cottage itself, though fairly spacious by standards of its time, was lacking in all the most basic amenities familiar to urban dwellers. It faced directly into the prevailing nor'westerlies which howled in from Greenland at all seasons. There was no porch to mitigate the effect of the elements on the front door. There were no dormer windows upstairs to defy the gales, no running water, no inside toilet and no electric light. These all came much later, at my mother's insistence. Water was carried into the house in enamel buckets from the wee burn alongside the croft steadings. Light, and indeed some of the heat in the living room, came from a hissing Tilley. In the bedrooms, cotton wick paraffin lamps had by then supplanted their ancestors, the centuries-old cruisies, though the general principal was the same.

The golden picture-postcard sweep of Sangobeag sands, so popular with Scottish calendar publishers, provided an ideal playground, conjoined as it was to our croft. Life was anything but romantic for my father, especially during the eight or nine months of the year he plied his trade as a lobster fisherman. It was a matter of running fast to stand still, governed as it was by weather conditions, wireless forecasts and tides. I remember well lying snug in bed at three o'clock on bitter winter mornings, hearing my father rise to catch the tide and haul in his creels. On one occasion he and his boatmates chanced upon a grimmer haul – bodies from a naval frigate torpedoed off Cape Wrath in 1944. From June to August, when the weather was too warm for lobsters to travel live from Durness to Billingsgate Market in London, the fishing boat was hauled in for its annual tarring and painting. After that, it was time to cut, dry and take home the peats, shear the sheep, scythe, stack and store the hay. The peats arrived three miles from the moss in a cart drawn by our old mare Beaut, while the hay was transported in the same manner to the three little barns it took to hold all the winter fodder. Life on a croft revolves as much around the welfare of its animals as of its human inhabitants. The mare, the two cows, the 60-odd lambing ewes, the hens, the occasional pig, the sheepdog and the many cats, all had to be provided for. We were largely self-sufficient in food. War shortages, apart from sweets and fruit, rarely affected our little corner. We killed our own sheep or pigs, grew our own potatoes and turnips, collected our own eggs, milked our own cows. There was always a firkin of salt herring in the barn, while the saithe my father caught for lobster-bait was also part of our diet.

Religion played a significant part in our lives. We attended the parish church regularly from an early age and my father's evening ritual before retiring to bed was to read aloud a chapter from the Bible. At school we learned by rote the entire Shorter Catechism, several of the more common Scottish Metrical Psalms, together with salient chapters of the Bible.

I was nearly six before I went to school in Durness. My mother had taught me to read reasonably fluently in the months beforehand. Highlights of the school year were the annual festive season party, referred to as 'the Christmas Tree', Sutherland Provincial Mod, held in Golspie, Dornoch, Lairg or Brora on the first Friday of June, and the school bus trip at the beginning of the summer holidays to Inverness, in the green luxury Bedford OB coach owned by Burr's of Tongue.

I was fated to witness the sad decline of the last remnant of an ancient Gaelic culture which survived the Viking settlers in North-West Sutherland. When I was born, the majority of adults in the community were still able to use the language as an everyday means of communication, although the last monoglot Gaelic speaker had long since died. Today perhaps half-a-dozen remaining elderly people speak it fluently. The death of the language in Durness was largely due to official indifference or indeed hostility from officialdom of the early twentieth century, while well-meaning attempts to redress this in recent years have made little impact so far.

My childhood came to an end when I left Durness at the age of twelve to continue my formal education at Dornoch Academy, in the tiny, ancient Sutherland capital. Though I have lived in various towns and cities, and travelled to many odd corners of the world, I still regard the croft cottage in Sangobeag as my spiritual home, and I remember my childhood with fondness and gratitude for the experience.'

(Memories of Sangobeag reproduced here by kind permission of Willie Morrison.)

Opposite: The few buildings and small harbour belonging to the privately owned Rispond Lodge Estate blend into the rocky landscape adjacent to a safe, although somewhat shallow and tide-dependent anchorage on the western lip of Loch Eriboll. Rispond House (centre) dates from 1788 and in what is now the eastern wing of the house salmon were once processed and packed into jars for export. Around the jetty is a group of buildings formerly associated with the all-important seaborne trade: customs house, chandlery, salt cellar, coopers' sheds, net loft and three-storied crow-stepped store (topped with a weathervane in the shape of a salmon) dating from *c*.1750. There is a feeling of great antiquity here, and tales are told of the first ever export of salted herring from Scotland to St Petersburg *c*.1825. In late Victorian times the entrepreneurial Robert Garden (of whom more later) established a store at Rispond, sending supplies from Orkney by his boat the SS *Cormorant*, which became a familiar sight at this little 'port' for the Durness area.

Stunning coastal scenery at Ceannabienne, looking across the mouth of Loch Eriboll towards the gleaming cliffs of Whiten Head. To the Vikings it was *Hvitr* ('the White Headland'); the Celts named it *Kennageall* ('the Headland of the Stranger') as Haco, defeated at Largs, finally set sail for home around the headland. The history of these northern coastal lands is one of clearance and resettlement. The census of 1841 recorded ten families living at Ceannabienne. Although the initial attempt failed, the small township was cleared shortly thereafter, and now only close examination of the landscape reveals evidence of previous occupation.

Until the 1930s, the Heilam ferry (Portnancon to Ard Neakie) carried foot passengers a mile across Loch Eriboll, saving eleven miles around the lochside road. The fifteen foot sailing boat also called on demand at Eriboll and Kempie. The ferry had originally operated from Port Chamuill nearby, but about 1889 the pier was built at Portnancon ('Port of the Dogs') where the ferryman's house doubled as an inn, and a store (also known as the customs house) stocked essentials brought in by sea. 'Puffers' delivered coal for local distribution by horse and cart. Fjord-like Loch Eriboll extends ten miles inland and is one of the finest deep water anchorages around our coasts; during the Second World War Atlantic and Russian convoys assembled here. HMS *Hood* – the supreme symbol of Britain's naval power – sailed from the loch in 1941 shortly before her fatal encounter with the German warship *Bismarck*. Sunk off Greenland with the loss of 1,416 lives (all the crew except for three) she was the biggest single naval loss of the war. Stones set in the hillside above the pier spell out the name HMS *Hood* – an appropriately poignant memorial tended annually by local schoolchildren, and a reminder that the ship's company had spent their last shore leave on British soil at Portnancon before *Hood* sailed to her doom.

Established in the 1830s following the evictions, the small township of Laid extends along the line of the hillside above the western shore of Loch Eriboll. Looking across to Eilean Choraidh (left) and photographed about 80 years ago, this house, No. 107 Laid, is set amid byres on the lochside and surrounded by immaculately constructed dry-stane enclosures, features which make good use of the plentiful supply of the raw material so readily available in the rocky terrain hereabouts. The owner told me that the house dates from 1898 and at one stage had been occupied by fifteen people! The single-track road was metalled in 1953, and electricity arrived only twenty years ago.

Having crossed the River Polla at the head of the loch, the entrance to the Eriboll Estate (established 1870) is soon reached, and immediately opposite is a famous red telephone box. According to *The Times* of 13 June 1992, this was the last A and B button payphone in mainland Britain, and the picture accompanying the report shows several cameramen and sound recordists grouped around the kiosk, perhaps trying to record the message 'Press button B and try again later' for the last time! Eriboll Church stands quite alone and is now 200 years old although still in good heart and used for occasional services. The interior is furnished with old pews and lit by candles, but the finial shown mounted on the far end of the roof in this photograph now lies broken in two pieces on the ground. Hopefully someone will feel compelled to rectify this, if for no other reason than to mark the bicentenary of this simple but delightful building.

Ard Neakie is an amazing land formation consisting of two identical curving beaches which form a narrow isthmus to a spit of land protruding into Loch Eriboll. Until the Second World War the Heilam ferry carried foot passengers, including their bicycles, from here to Portnancon directly opposite across the loch. The former ferryman's house and inn dates from the 1830s. In late Victorian times a limestone quarry on the promontory fuelled four well-built lime kilns which lie adjacent to the jetty. The inn's license to sell alcohol was revoked 'to save quarrymen from temptation'.

Above: The River Hope runs out to the sea at the northern end of Loch Eriboll and, a century ago, travellers would necessarily have crossed the river by ferry in order to continue their onward journey to Tongue. The small chain ferry boat, ferryman's house and Hope Lodge on the hill are grouped together in this picture, which dates from *c.*1903 and is No. 2 in a postcard series issued by Robert Garden and sold through his mainland stores. The ferry has long been replaced by a bridge built to the left of the former ferry-house. *Below:* Built in the last quarter of the nineteenth century, the sporting lodge at Hope has interesting architectural features including an ornamental turret and integral verandahs. Well screened by trees today, the views were comparatively unobstructed at one time.

Some claim the view from Hope Lodge up the loch towards Ben Hope (3,040 feet) to be the finest in Sutherland. Windswept and barren, the towering mountain – the most northerly Munro – is set in immense, desolate moorland country which serves to emphasise through force of perspective a deeper significance and presence than the mountain would have in a more crowded landscape. Noted for rare Alpine plants, Ben Hope has become something of a legend in the far north for here in 1885, Professor M. F. Heddle, an Edinburgh geologist returning from South Africa, found Scotland's first diamond – reported to be a gem of hand-sized dimensions.

The ruins of Dun Dornaigil (or Dun Dornadilla) stand close to the road in Strathmore three miles beyond the southern end of Loch Hope. Concentrations of such early defensive buildings occur in Skye, Caithness, Orkney and Shetland. Hollow, light dry-stone walls allowed them to be built to considerable heights and they have no counterpart outside Scotland or, more particularly, outside the Highlands and Islands. I believe that the triangular lintel above the doorway, illustrated here, would have absorbed well the competing directional thrusts of the weighty stonework. The techniques of the early builders worldwide never cease to surprise and deserve our respect; this dun, the best preserved in Sutherland, has stood for 2,000 years.

The ruins of Moin House stand at the highest point of the bleak moorland road across 'the deep and dangerous morass of the Moin' between Hope and Tongue. In 1830, while constructing the road at his own expense, the Marquis of Stafford (1st Duke of Sutherland) financed the building of this refuge for travellers. *Top:* Following the evictions from Strathmore, Melness House, overlooking the Kyle of Tongue, became the hub of an extensive sheep farming enterprise in mid-Victorian times. In those days, when most trade along this coast was conducted by sea, Melness and Talmine were the focus for fishing smacks, general cargo and pilot boats, while high quality stone and slate were exported through the little harbour at nearby Port Vasgo. *Above:* The old ferry house at Achuvoldrach is a forlorn sight today: the little circular building is now roofless and the viewing opening on the kyle side is blocked up. Many must have been thankful to have found shelter here while awaiting the ferry in times past. Both photographs date from *c*.1934 and show the many-peaked profile of Ben Loyal (2,504 feet) known as 'the Queen of Scottish mountains'.

The House of Tongue, the watchtower and signal station (centre), and Tongue Lodge *c.*1903. The 200 year old hexagonal watchtower on the Tongue (east) side of the kyle provided, as at Achuvoldrach, a shelter and waiting-room for those taking the ferry. The alternative to the mile-wide crossing was a ten mile road journey via Kinloch. At ebb tide the Kyle of Tongue is a wilderness of sand and shallow water, and in 1971 a causeway and bridge were built across the small island in mid-channel linking the two former ferry points.

The battles and rivalries of the Mackays and Sutherlands largely comprise the history of the county. The Lordship of Reay, the principal branch of the Mackays, held lands in the north and west for almost 600 years, and the House of Tongue – one of the major houses of the north coast – is an ancient seat of Clan Mackay. The present building dates from 1678, while an earlier tower house nearby was demolished in 1830. Financial reverses resulted in the sale of the Reay Estates in 1829: the purchaser was the Sutherland Estate which, by this simple monetary transaction, gained what it had failed to achieve during three centuries of warfare. The elaborately stone-built, crow-stepped and double doored eighteenth century boathouse by the shore has a little piece of history all of its own (see page 78).

Although more than 90 years have passed since his death, the name of Robert Garden remains a legend along these northern coasts. Born in 1846, his early commercial experience consisted variously of work on the farm, being apprenticed to a boot and shoemaker, and receiving training as a slater. Unable to settle, but still a relatively young man, he arrived in Kirkwall in 1873 from his native Aberdeenshire armed with a plan of action. In those far-off days, shops in rural localities were few and far between except in the larger towns, and in the remotest areas consumers suffered from a lack of variety of goods. Additionally, in a non-competitive environment, local shopkeepers could impose charges at will on the resident population. Garden's arrival in Orkney coincided with the gradual improvement of the road system, and his plan was simple: with horse and van he would call on these outlying communities with what was initially a limited range of groceries for sale at a modest profit. Simultaneously he would purchase from his customers their fresh produce – butter, eggs and vegetables – which he would then sell on. Through the convenience and regularity of his rounds, the increasingly varied stock he brought to the door, and in the straightforwardness of his dealings, he earned the trust and respect of his clientele. His entrepreneurial spirit and restless energy seemed limitless, and soon his evolving empire necessitated the establishment of several remote satellite depots supported by a head office in Kirkwall.

If such success could be generated on mainland Orkney, what, Garden thought, might he not do for the many islands and small locations further afield in Orkney and Shetland – and even Fair Isle? By 1884 he was implementing his concept of floating shops, bringing goods from Kirkwall to the islands in specially converted boats fitted out in sections for grocery, drapery and animal foodstuffs. These vessels tied up at the nearest jetty or, where none existed, anchored in the bay so that potential buyers could be ferried from the shore to select goods aboard. The venture never looked back and proved to be a springboard for the next phase of his developing strategy. This involved bringing the benefits of provisioning by his Kirkwall boats to the north coast of Sutherland, about which more will be said shortly.

Photographs of Robert Garden in Sutherland are virtually unknown. He is seen here with Mrs Garden in the grounds of Dunvarrich, the house he built in conjunction with his store at Tongue. The car, bearing an original Sutherland 'NS' registration prefix, was registered in Garden's name as new in April 1904, but was transferred in November 1905. The Baby Peugeot with red paintwork was the first car in Tongue. (Photograph reproduced here by kind permission of Peter Burr, and by arrangement with the Skerray Historical Association.)

By the end of Queen Victoria's reign, Robert Garden had established an extensive trading presence along the coast of North Sutherland and as far south as Loch Broom. Within this area I spoke to many about his activities, and while most recollections had been handed down and some conflicted on particular aspects, all agreed on the importance of Garden's contribution to sustaining communities in the North-West. One described him as a wheeler-dealer and shrewd businessman who conducted often complicated business dealings informally, usually with nothing in writing; such deals might typically be sealed with a handshake in an age when a man's word was his bond. His stores, purely functional buildings of corrugated iron and wood, have now for the most part simply mouldered away due to the passage of time. One written source states that Bettyhill was Garden's first Sutherland store, while someone to whom I spoke was adamant that Melvich, nearest to Orkney, took premier place. His outlets were tied, with the individual operators trading under their own names and paying rent to Garden who supplied them monthly with goods shipped from Kirkwall, initially by the SS *Aberdeen* and, from 1898 to 1932, by the *Cormorant* (above). A sturdy boat, she sailed in all weathers and was worked hard, earning her keep wherever she could as the Garden philosophy was that an empty boat on the high seas was a financial liability. When not replenishing the various stores, *Cormorant* was running loads often on a barter or swap basis – perhaps a cargo of wool-clippings, the payment for which might be a load of coal. Another recalled her particularly high-pitched whistle, which was sounded on arrival at her ports of call. From varying sources I have compiled a list of these calling-places (east to west): Melvich, Skerray (to include Bettyhill), Tongue (and Melness), Laid, Rispond (for Durness), Kinlochbervie, Scourie, Ardvar (annually to collect wool), Loch Nedd (for Drumbeg), Culkein (for Achnacarnin), Lochinver (for Mackay's shop) and Badentarbet (for Achiltibuie). At one time the annual wool-clippings from Island Roan may also have been handled by *Cormorant*.

Supplies delivered for the stores included groceries, boots and shoes, clothing, a range of hardware, items for the croft (hand tools, nails, lamps and fence posts) and vehicle parts (dynamos, fan belts etc.). Loads carried included peat, coal, timber, stone and slate, wool, salted herring, lobsters, whelks, winkles, bolls of meal and flour, and sheep. Wheat and barley were collected for grinding at Garden's Orkney mill and returned to the Sutherland stores for resale. (Photograph reproduced here by kind permission of Alastair Cormack.)

Robert Garden built Dunvarrich in 1894 in order to provide living accommodation for one of his two sons, who operated his most prestigious mainland store. This lay 200 yards away from the house but is out of sight in this *c*.1903 picture. From the supply aspect, the properties were located conveniently only a mile from the jetties on the Kyle of Tongue. The house – built of local granite – looks towards Ben Loyal, the source of the quarried stone; local information suggests that in the very early days the quarrymaster himself resided here for a time. This view, captioned 'Dun Varrich House' and published by Robert Garden, is appropriately No. 1 in his postcard series, which was sold through the adjoining Tongue store.

Described by *The Orcadian* at the peak of his business life as 'Orkney's premier merchant prince', Robert Garden died in 1912 at the age of 66 years, leaving by the standards of his day an immense fortune. On the day of his funeral, flags flew at half mast on public buildings and on all vessels in Kirkwall harbour. Members of his staff carried the coffin to his grave in the churchyard of St Magnus Cathedral, and there was general recognition that Kirkwall would not see his like again. Less publicly at Tongue, Dunvarrich was vacated (this photograph is captioned 'The Flitting') and Garden's belongings made ready for their return to Orkney via Scrabster Pier. If one era had ended another was about to begin, for Peter Burr who had operated the Garden store on Shapinsay moved here to rent the Tongue enterprise, which also included a small shop at Melness. In 1932 he bought out the business, still known as Burr's of Tongue to this day, from Garden's successors. (Photograph reproduced here by kind permission of Peter Burr and by arrangement with the Skerray Historical Association.)

Two 'between the wars' interior photographs of Burr's of Tongue. The fittings are reminiscent of a past era, and the shelves are well-stocked with a variety of mouth-watering delicacies. This was an age when personal service and attention were paramount; a chair is thoughtfully provided for the convenience of customers waiting to have their purchases weighed and wrapped. In the upper picture, Fiona MacKenzie is seen behind the counter. Other parts of this former Garden store included a bakery and stockrooms. Externally, there was ample room for the vehicles required to conduct the extensive mobile trade, which included the north coast mail-carrying contract to Thurso. Before me is a postcard addressed to Helmsdale and franked Tongue, 25 December 1905 and Thurso, 26 December. In those days absolutely nothing was allowed to impede the progress of the mail. (Photographs reproduced here by kind permission of Peter Burr and by arrangement with the Skerray Historical Association.)

Two generations of the Burr family – Peter and son Norman – with an early commercial vehicle *c*.1920. Purchased as an engine and chassis only, Peter Burr employed a local joiner to construct the cab. As his grandson (also Peter) told me recently, the joiner specialised in the building of outside toilets, and the pedigree is self-evident! Yes, I see exactly what he means . . . (Photograph reproduced here by kind permission of Peter Burr.)

The mere mention of Castle Varrich should induce a note of caution, for the only certainty is that its origins and possible uses are shrouded from us in the mists of the distant past. The existing ruins are generally thought most likely to be those of an early Mackay stronghold. More definitely, the man standing on the shore *c*.1908 has been identified as H. MacDonald.

ESTABLISHED CHURCH, TONGUE
(RENOVATED 1680. BURIAL PLACE OF LORDS OF REAY)

St Andrew's Church, substantially rebuilt by Donald Mackay, Master of Reay in 1680, stands on the site of a much earlier place of worship. Under the crow-stepped west gable, surmounted by a bellcote, steps provide access to the laird's loft above the Mackay burial vault. Sadly, the particularly fine carved wooden loft canopy dating from 1680 was removed in 1951 to the National Museum in Edinburgh. The Reay family still retain the right of burial here.

TONGUE HOTEL, SUTHERLAND. N. B. JOHN MACKENZIE, PROPRIETOR

Leafing through the small brochure issued by the Tongue Hotel during the period of John Mackenzie's proprietorship, images leap from the pages which leave a lasting impression. In the drawing and private sitting rooms are deep, comfortable chairs and sofas with large cushions, tall glass-fronted display cabinets filled with interesting-looking china, framed pictures adorn the walls, and plant fronds cascade from ornamental pots. The dining room is graced by a large sideboard, carved and sturdy wooden chairs upholstered in leather, and neatly laid tables covered with fine napery. The brochure proclaims that 'the hotel is splendidly furnished throughout' and that 'every effort is made to provide home comforts for visiting guests'. A large farm operated in conjunction with the hotel 'ensured a plentiful supply of fresh butter, milk and eggs'. Baths, all-day fires or evening fires attracted additional charges; visitors' servants could be accommodated in the Stewards' Room. Externally, there was garaging for over twenty cars, and Shell petrol and oils were available, together with grease and tyres. A large charabanc was available for picnic parties, and visitors could hire a capable driver with a vehicle from the hotel's fleet of 'first class motor cars'. Maybe one of these is seen here surrounded by an admiring group, while from the brochure I have selected this photograph of the glass-covered entrance hall, *c*.1913. The Tongue Hotel would have been the finest along the North Sutherland coast at this time.

Situated north-east of Tongue and under the spectacular ramparts of Watch Hill, Coldbackie has an enviable view across the kyle towards Melness where an extraordinary drama was played out in March 1746. A sloop, the *Hazard*, carrying more than £13,000 in gold from France destined for the army of Prince Charles Edward Stuart (and considerably off her intended course for Inverness), ran aground at Ard Skinid, just south of the Rabbit Islands, after hot pursuit by the frigate *Sheerness*. The gold was spirited ashore under cover of darkness to begin an overland journey to Inverness, but the local militia, supported by crew from the *Sheerness*, engaged the Jacobites and recovered the bullion at Lochan Hakel near Kinloch. The prisoners taken were secured temporarily in the boathouse below Tongue House, mentioned earlier. For the Jacobite forces, the denial of funds intended for food and pay proved a key factor in their defeat three weeks later on Drummossie Muir, as surviving letters written by the Young Pretender confirm.

I took the track to the well-built harbour at Skullomie, which lies on the eastern shore of Tongue Bay, to see where, in the distant past, the islanders from Eilean nan Ron (Island Roan) had landed by boat after a three mile crossing to attend church at Strathtongue. Their journey continued on foot through fields and woods near the burn for over a mile until the church door (on the right of this *c*.1932 photograph) was reached. The church was built after the Disruption of 1843 and the first minister appointed in 1847. Initially the congregation was drawn from a wide area, including Skerray, and there was capacity for perhaps 500 worshippers. The two-storied manse (obscured by the church) was sold in 1939, while the church, which closed about 1950, is now used as a storeroom by current owners Michael Keitch and his wife, who provide bed and breakfast at the former manse.

Although Eilean nan Ron ('Island of Seals'), more commonly known as Island Roan, lies about a mile from the mainland at the nearest point, the rocky coast and high cliffs made access far from easy. Fishing and crofting were the mainstays of the economy on this 700 acre island which once supported a peak population of about 80 residents. After continuous occupation for about 120 years in the modern era, the island was evacuated in December 1938. While depopulation followed by evacuation and final abandonment are not unusual around our coasts, experience elsewhere suggests that for those directly involved – especially the older generation – the tragedy is compounded by feelings of failure and rootlessness resulting from an inability to adjust to a totally alien way of life on the mainland. For those wishing more detailed information, an excellent little history is available from Skerray Post Office. Could this picture show the final class at Island Roan School? Cathy Ann Mackay, pupil-teacher, is pictured working with her brothers, Donald John (thirteen years) and John Angus (fifteen years), the school's last pupils. The building is now a ruin. (Photograph reproduced here by kind permission of the Skerray Historical Association.)

A smart turnout for the photographer by the boys and girls of Skerray School in 1924, with E. Ewing, headmaster (right), and Mrs J. Telford. The school closed in 1972.

Situated between Tongue Bay and the Borgie River, this is a superb portrayal of a linear crofting development at Lotts (Skerray), as captured by a photographer in the 1930s. There is a mix of traditional buildings (some thatched), while the proximity of the surrounding neatly-worked croftland and conical haystacks emphasise the hand of Man working in harmony with Nature. Peat was commonly used as a source of fuel at this time.

Skerray pier, with Robert Garden's former store and bakery (foreground), and Island Roan in the background. This was an important port of call for the *Cormorant* which supplied both the Skerray and Bettyhill stores. Owing to the unsuitability of the jetty at Torrisdale Bay, supplies were delivered onwards by horse and cart over Apigill to Bettyhill. Stockan, an Orcadian, operated the Skerray bakery in the early days. Tods of Orkney purchased Robert Garden's business in 1912, and manufacture the internationally famous (and delicious) Orkney oatcakes which still bear the Stockan name. Virtually no trace remains of the old store today, and the melodious whistle sounded by *Cormorant* as she nosed into the bay is now but a memory for a few of long ago.

At Borgie Bridge, according to Baddeley's *Thorough Guide* for 1885, eastbound travellers had a choice of route to Bettyhill. The carriage road climbed over Apigill, descending to a chain-ferry which crossed the Naver one and a quarter miles from the Bettyhill Inn. However, more detailed instructions were necessary for those on foot wishing to save two or three miles. They were advised to follow the road along the west side of the River Borgie (past the Lodge, pictured *c.*1920), and after two miles cross the river by a footbridge near Crossburn farm. The guide goes on: 'Hence the path continues east some distance and then is lost in hillocky ground. The sand-dunes, however, on the west side of the strath are quickly reached, and a descent made over them to the ferry, beyond which, on the brow of the hill is seen the comfortable Bettyhill Inn.' This ferry, described as being 'beneath the inn' has long since vanished, while the chain-boat ferry further up the strath was subsequently replaced by a narrow road bridge. Memories of past days are still perpetuated by a property close to the bridge which, although named 'The Ferry House', has replaced that shown in the lower photograph.

A minor road to Skelpick along the east bank of the Naver gives access to a number of prehistoric sites including hut circles, brochs and chambered cairns. Those having more general interests might visit Achanlochy to view the site of one of the many small communities which thrived prior to the notorious early nineteenth century Strathnaver Clearances. Typical buildings were longhouses constructed of stone and peat where people and their cattle lived in adjoining sections under a roof of turf and thatch. Smoke from a peat fire in the middle of the bare floor escaped through a hole in the roof. An excellent model of Achanlochy may be seen at the Strathnaver Museum. The 'age of improvement' swept away such communities as land was cleared to make way for more profitable sheep; the displaced population was resettled along the coast. Later, sporting lodges sprung up in the strath, as here at Skelpick. (This *c*.1903 view is No. 11 in the Robert Garden series of postcards.)

Further inland up Strathnaver at Skail is a memorial cairn 'to commemorate the place where the first gathering of men of the 93rd Sutherland Highlanders took place on formation of the regiment in September 1800'. Six hundred men were raised within a few weeks, and the 93rd accumulated a distinguished record of service in the Crimea (where they formed the famous 'thin red line' at Balaclava), the West Indies, Canada and India where members of this most Highland of regiments were awarded seven Victoria Crosses for their valour at the relief of Lucknow. Men to be fêted by a grateful nation, you might think? No, the reality was that many returned to the soil of their birth to find their families evicted and their homes in ruins.

In 1819 the Sutherland Estate built a coaching inn at Bettyhill which expanded over the years to become firstly a small hotel, and subsequently the more familiar building seen today (photographs *c.*1905 and 1935 respectively). The site was well-chosen; the view from the windows is stupendous. The Naver runs to the sea in Torrisdale Bay, another of the natural wonders of this coast where, in an immense accumulation of sand uncommon mountain plants flourish almost to sea level. The earliest Christian settlement hereabouts is on Eilean Neave (also known as Coombe Island, background). 'During World War II, King Haakon VII of Norway was a frequent visitor to this hotel' proclaims a notice on the wall by reception. Norway was then under German occupation, and clandestine operations in support of the underground movement there were being actively undertaken from Shetland ('the Shetland Bus'); from Bettyhill the King was very probably giving secret encouragement and maintaining contact with his compatriots based there during those years.

The surface is metalled now, but Pier Road (upper picture) still provides a pleasant stroll to the track which finally drops down to the jetty on Torrisdale Bay. The navigable channels through the sandy, tidal shallows require care, making the landing here suitable for only the smallest of vessels. Both photographs bear the publisher's date-code of 1914.

Registration plate NS 10, previously seen on Robert Garden's car in the grounds of Dunvarrich ten years earlier, makes a reappearance, although this is a very different vehicle having capacity at the rear to carry passengers and parcels. Photographed outside Bettyhill Post Office in 1914, this was one of the Albions taken over by Burr's of Tongue, and on this occasion is perhaps undertaking a mail run to Thurso.

Cattlefield *c*.1920. By 1815, after the resettlement which followed the initial Strathnaver Clearances, land holdings in Bettyhill had increased sevenfold from fourteen to 98. The official policy of allocating the incomers small-sized plots along the coast was a calculated attempt to force crofters into other activities, especially fishing, even though most had never previously set foot in a boat. The black roof of Robert Garden's old Bettyhill store, identified by a local resident of long-standing, can be seen in the distance (right of centre).

The Scottish Education Act passed in 1872 was from the outset more comprehensive than the English counterpart, requiring the election of school boards in every burgh and parish and making school attendance compulsory throughout the country for children aged between five and fourteen years. Bettyhill School is a type of building familiar throughout this book – solidly constructed of stone with crow-stepped gables and those distinctive chimney stacks. In this pre-First World War photograph the pupils take a break, while in the adjoining well-cultivated garden there is ample evidence that the headmaster kept bees. The school looks across to surrounding hills and is set above Farr Bay in sight of Clachan Church (extreme right). Such a setting must have acted as a potent force on the imaginations of these young children.

The Church of St Columba was built in the late eighteenth century, although this religious site dates back another 1,000 years as evidenced by the famous Farr Stone which stands within the walled burial ground facing west. At one time the church, which had internal galleries (now removed), could reputedly accommodate a congregation of 1,500 people and was notable as a focal point during the Clearances. Made redundant in the 1950s, St Columba's is now the home of the Strathnaver Museum which, although specialising in aspects relating to the Clearances and crofting, has a wide range of other interesting exhibits. The late Dr Ian Grimble (author, historian, broadcaster and a keen supporter of the museum), who first came to Bettyhill in 1946, found a community with qualities of humanity and simple friendliness. 'In those days the village was so poor it existed on virtually a barter economy but neighbours helped each other as a matter of course. Grimble always felt they were in closer touch with the fundamentals of life than any other people he had ever met.' (Obituary, *The Times*, 19 January 1995.)

Sheep on the hill look down towards the church on the valley floor which, by a neat twist, has since become a museum dedicated to the Clearances which made way for *them*. There is considerable depth to this well-composed *c*.1935 photograph of Clachan, where the road spirals upwards over the distant hill and onwards to Strathy and Melvich. Immediately beyond the museum is the former manse of the Revd David Mackenzie whose part in the 1819 evictions has been seen by some as equivocal. Today, in the former group of agricultural buildings on the roadside (right), is Elizabeth's Cafe, combined with a Tourist Information Centre; welcome facilities along this sparsely populated coast.

Situated eight miles from Clachan, Strathy is a scattered crofting community whose little population was swollen by a factor of ten (to 40) following resettlement in the early nineteenth century. The new holdings then allocated consisted of narrow strips of land which averaged less than two acres apiece, the inadequacies of which would manifest themselves subsequently by years of shortage and, at worst, famine. Once there were four churches here; this is another building of note – the inn, pictured *c*.1912. A figurehead from the 262 ton Norwegian barque *Thorwaldsen*, built in Trondhjem in 1844, may be seen at the Strathnaver Museum. She foundered off Strathy Point on 9 March 1858 with the loss of eight lives; surviving timbers are known to have been incorporated into local houses.

Initially the road to Kirtomy squeezes through a steep-sided miniature ravine before descending to croftland enclosed by two ridges of a valley facing north towards the sea. Kirtomy is a gem of this coast, and at Kirtomy Mains (top) I met Neil Mackay who has lived all his life in this crofting and fishing community. Sat in his front porch we spoke not of 'cabbages and kings' but of kale and millstones! During the First World War 40 local men had enlisted in various branches of the navy, and remarkably all had returned safely. Until the Second World War, Kirtomy kale had been famous and in keen demand. This entirely local variety grew about eighteen inches high with a very large purple head, but was lost forever by the failure one year to retain seed for the following year's planting. From a quarry on the eastern ridge (above) rock was cut for millstones, some even exported by sea through Scrabster to Australia. The last of these three-foot by one-foot stones with a central hole still lies by the roadside (abandoned where it fell damaged perhaps 90 years ago, and clearly visible between two byres at the bend in the road in the lower (*c.*1930) photograph). Now contained within the boundary of a more recently built house there, the stone is a tangible reminder of an industry now largely forgotten.

The road from Strathy provides tantalising glimpses of Bighouse Head and, increasingly towards Melvich, the outlines of Orkney emerge from a distant haze of blue. The Melvich Hotel, a favourite with sportsmen since Victorian times, looks towards the headland and stands where the minor road serving Portskerra joins the main highway; these crofting and fishing settlements are contiguous. Although a date-stone of 1895 appears on one elevation, the oldest part of the building may date from the 1830s. The hotel lay on the Tongue to Thurso coach route (a distance of 46 miles taking 7 ¾ hours in 1885), the mail cart leaving Melvich daily at noon for Thurso, eighteen miles distant (fare 2/3d). These two photographs show the hotel and the indifferent state of the road *c*.1910, and (below) a rear view from the garden *c*.1930 which illustrates well how the building had grown by subsequent additions.

Portskerra scenes 1905–1930. Many little settlements along the north coast are individually served by minor roads branching from the main highway; each community goes about its own self-contained business on land and sea. Most have poor harbours, but all face the treacherous northern seas where powerful currents and sudden squalls make fishing in open boats a hazardous occupation. 'The only safe haven between Loch Eriboll and Caithness is the port of eternity' is an old saying. All these communities can tell tales of suffering – the tragedy of lost boats and loss of life – and Portskerra is no exception.

One August evening in 1918 several boats were fishing for herring in the bay when a severe gale struck within minutes from the north-west turning a previously calm sea into a seething maelstrom. While some crews eventually made the shore through huge breakers, one boat was overwhelmed with the loss of four lives in the mouth of the River Halladale, while three others drowned as their boat was smashed on the rocks of Bighouse Head. The tragedy touched everyone in this tiny community, and in recent years a memorial has been raised above Portskerra Pier.

In the days of the clans, Strath Halladale was a line of demarcation for competing spheres of influence; Bighouse, another great house of the Sutherland coast, is a former seat of a major branch of Clan Mackay. Built on a spit of land in the mouth of the River Halladale within sound of the sea, the house dates from the 1760s. The river sweeps around three sides of the property, a site which is apparently frivolously referred to by locals as *An Torr* ('the heap'). Much further back in time the name Bighouse may have originated from the Norse *Bygghus*, meaning 'barley house' or 'barn'. *Top:* The group of buildings include the mansion house (right), pictured here *c.*1910 incorporating at the rear a walled garden with two-storied pavilion surmounted by a salmon-shaped weathervane. Such interesting ornamentation previously encountered at Rispond (page 65), and the adjoining salmon-fishing station and icehouse, are clues to the original source of wealth here. Much uncertainty surrounds the history of the building on the left, named 'Barracks', which may have originally stood at another location and been dismantled and re-erected here. The lower picture shows the view from the walled garden *c.*1930.

Although the Celts were a warrior people and many of their leisure activities were naturally rooted in trials of strength, speed and stamina, they also had a great love of music, song and dance. The 'Forty-five', the Highland Clearances and emigration forced successive generations of Scots overseas, and while for the most part they arrived abroad destitute with little more than the clothes they wore, they nevertheless remained true to their culture and memories of home. Wherever Scots settled their culture accompanied them, and the annual Highland Games is an important part of that heritage, where competitions such as hill racing, putting the stone, throwing the hammer and tug-of-war stand side by side with piping and Highland dancing. Today, Highland Gatherings are found across the globe – in Europe, Africa, Asia, Australia, Canada and the United States – where every state in the Union stages an annual games incorporating traditional events and local variations. The largest and most famous is the Grandfather Mountain Games, a four day jamboree in North Carolina, and a far cry indeed from the Strath Halladale Games, photographed here *c.*1937. For many, tossing the caber (a length of tree trunk) is still a highlight. But, did it go over?

Long ago drovers would move their cattle from the coastal gathering grounds around Melvich and Bighouse through Strath Halladale to the trysts further south. Twenty-one miles inland, south of Halladale Bridge and beyond Forsinard and the Achentoul Forest, is Kinbrace, a handful of houses in the middle of nowhere, seen here *c.*1905. This area is part of the vast, lonely wilderness of Sutherland and neighbouring Caithness known as the Flow Country, a tract of blanket bog one million acres in extent. These peatlands are the habitat of rare birds and animals and startling coloured mosses and bog flowers, including insect-devouring sundew plants. Opened in 1874, the railway line financed by the Highland Railway and the Duke of Sutherland snakes through the desolate landscape – north to Thurso and Wick and south to Helmsdale. Building material for the early houses in Kinbrace arrived courtesy of the railway. Winters here can be severe, and in February 2001 passengers stranded for six hours on a train buried in snowdrifts ten feet high were eventually rescued by workers from the 23,000 acre Borrobol Estate using an ex-army Sno-cat. Occasionally Kinbrace features in weather reports, usually when temperatures have plummeted to some record-breaking new low.

Fishermen tend to exaggerate the size of 'the one that got away'; equally, they are adept at offering excuses for *not* catching fish: the level of the loch is too high/ low; conditions are too bright/cloudy; the water is too warm/cold; the wind is excessive or insufficient, or, more ingeniously, from the wrong direction. Then there are the various flies . . . Loch Badanloch (pictured *c.*1918) is in 'the empty quarter' between Kinbrace and Strathnaver. (Photograph Christopher J. Uncles Collection; © The Wick Society.)

Centre: Monarchs of the Glen. (Photograph Christopher J. Uncles Collection; © The Wick Society.)

Left: 'I have been speechless – just drinking in – in a kind of soul rapture the delight of this life, the glorious stillness of this country, the majesty of its outline, the health in its atmosphere. The charm is inexpressible, isn't it, but it makes life with its sordidness and strife and struggle a thing of naught – it gives one a new life – the primitive life of God's first handiwork – nature – one stands aghast at one's lack of gratitude and misconception of its supreme delight.' (Millicent, Duchess of Sutherland (1867–1955) describing her surroundings at Loch Choire Lodge, 1899.)

On the far side of Ben Klibreck from Loch Choire Lodge lies Altnaharra ('Burn of the Sheiling') on Loch Naver. Here roads radiate to Lairg (via Crask), Hope (through Strathmore), Tongue, and Bettyhill (through Strathnaver). Following the clearance of Achness at the eastern end of Loch Naver, roof timbers and stonework from a redundant church there were incorporated into the building of the Altnaharra Inn. Pictured here *c*.1930, the serious fire of 1956 accounts for the changed appearance today. The hotel has extensive fishing interests and I was once shown their earliest fishing diary, a worn leather-bound volume of 1886.

Loch Naver, a major feature of the landscape, is six miles long and half a mile wide; its waters flow north through the strath to enter the sea in Torrisdale Bay at Bettyhill. The whole area, from the slopes of Ben Klibreck to the coast, supported a population of over 2,000 people divided into 50 small, vibrant communities prior to the Clearances, which started around Loch Choire in 1806 and continued in 1814 and 1819 in neighbouring Strathnaver. Throughout the strath large numbers of thatched dwellings and byres were put to the torch by the burning parties as, quite irrespective of circumstances, families were forced from their homes to marginal land at the coast.

The villain of the Strathnaver Clearances was Patrick Sellar, a Morayshire advocate employed as a legal agent by the Sutherland Estate, who personally supervised the evictions with enthusiasm and brutality. Brought to trial in 1816 for 'culpable homicide, oppression and real injury', he escaped conviction. The most detested man in Sutherland, Sellar became a successful sheep farmer ironically at Syre, his house not the later Victorian lodge shown here, but a more humble dwelling nearby, close to Syre Church.

The Donald Macleod memorial at Syre (Upper Strathnaver), opposite Rossal. 'The consternation and confusion were extreme; little or no time was given for the removal of persons or property; the people striving to remove the sick and the helpless before the fire should reach them; next, struggling to save the most valuable of their effects. The cries of the women and children, the roaring of the affrighted cattle, hunted at the same time by the yelling dogs of the shepherds amid the smoke and fire, altogether presented a scene that completely baffles description – it required to be seen to be believed. A dense cloud of smoke enveloped the whole country by day, and even extended far out to sea; at night an awfully grand but terrific scene presented itself – all the houses in an extensive district in flames at once. I myself ascended a height about eleven o'clock in the evening, and counted two hundred and fifty blazing houses, many of the owners of which were my relations, and all of whom I personally knew, but whose present condition – whether in or out of the flames – I could not tell. The conflagration lasted six days, till the whole of the dwellings were reduced to ashes or smoking ruins.'

Whole books have been devoted to the Sutherland Clearances, during which approximately 15,000 people were displaced, and only a flavour of this dark and turbulent period of Scottish history is possible here. Donald Macleod, a stonemason, witnessed the events of 1814 and his *Gloomy Memories* is but one account of the destruction of a way of life in this strath. Although 189 years may have passed since the folk departed from Rossal, their memory is kept alive by the surviving ruins of their simple buildings on the hillside above the River Naver.

Unsurprisingly, the Duke of Sutherland failed in his attempt in 1854 to raise further volunteers for the famous 93rd Regiment (see p82). One old man told the Duke how his forefathers had been deceived and 'that should the Czar of Russia take possession of Dunrobin Castle and Stafford House next term, that we could not expect worse treatment at his hands than we have experienced at the hands of your family for the last 50 years'.

Away to the south-east, atop Ben Bhraggie and overlooking Golspie and Dunrobin Castle (the ultimate symbol of Sutherland wealth and power) stands a huge statue to 'the most noble George Granville Leveson-Gower, second Marquis of Stafford and first Duke of Sutherland'. The monument faces the sea to which so many were committed as emigrants; the Duke's back is set firmly to the glens and straths so ruthlessly emptied in his name.